Farm Journal's
Speedy
Skillet
Meals

By Patricia A. Ward

Book Design
by Michael P. Durning

Illustrations
by Wendy Biggins

Farm Journal's
Speedy
Skillet
Meals

Farm Journal, Inc., Philadelphia, Pennsylvania

Other Farm Journal Cookbooks

Farm Journal's Country Cookbook
Farm Journal's Complete Pie Cookbook
Let's Start To Cook
Homemade Bread
America's Best Vegetable Recipes
Homemade Candy
Homemade Cookies
Homemade Ice Cream and Cake
Country Fair Cookbook
Great Home Cooking in America
Farm Journal's Homemade Snacks
Farm Journal's Best-Ever Recipes
Farm Journal's Great Dishes from the Oven
Farm Journal's Freezing and Canning Cookbook
Farm Journal's Friendly Food Gifts from Your Kitchen
Farm Journal's Choice Chocolate Recipes
Farm Journal's Cook It Your Way
Farm Journal's Complete Home Baking Book

Library of Congress Cataloging in Publication Data
Main entry under title: Farm journal's speedy skillet meals.
Includes index.
1. Skillet cookery. I. Ward, Patricia A.
II. Farm journal (Philadelphia, 1956-   )
TX840.S55F37   641.5'86   80-11179
ISBN 0-89795-009-7

Contents

Color
Photographs

Color Photographs by William Hazzard/Hazzard Studios

Introduction

Your skillet is one of the most versatile appliances in your kitchen—you can depend on it for frying, steaming, baking, grilling, poaching and panbroiling. Skillet cookery is quick, too; whether you choose a range-top skillet or an electric frypan, you'll save time, and often an entire meal can be cooked in one appliance.

Generations of country women treasured their black iron skillets, and with good reason—a well-seasoned skillet was a necessary utensil for cooking on a wood stove.

Although some cooks still turn to their tried-and-true iron skillets, there are many other practical and attractive alternatives: brightly colored electric woks; aluminum, tin, stainless steel and copper skillets of varying weights; and thermostatically-controlled electric frypans good-looking enough to bring to a buffet table. Each kind can be serviceable and efficient, so the skillet you choose depends on your individual preference.

When we asked the readers of Farm Journal magazine for their favorite skillet recipes last summer, the response from farm and ranch women all over the country was overwhelming. Many women told us they rely on skillet meals year 'round, but especially during the extra-busy planting and harvesting seasons. They sent us thousands of recipes, including extra-special breakfast omelets, stir-fried vegetable dishes, creamy seafood chowders and complete dinners-in-a-skillet. We sorted and categorized the recipes, then tested and perfected each one in our own Farm Journal Test Kitchens.

This book is divided into four sections: 30-Minute Specials,

Easy Stir-Fried Dishes, Family-style Favorites and Company-pleasing Specialties.

At the top of each recipe, we've given both the preparation time and the cooking time. Together, these figures will give you the total time needed to prepare and cook each recipe.

The preparation time listed in each recipe is an approximate guide—you might prepare the dish a bit faster or slower than the time given. Underneath the preparation time, you'll see the cooking time. This includes the amount of time needed to bring foods to a boil as well as the time needed to heat the oil or butter.

For successful results, we recommend using the size skillet or frypan indicated in each individual recipe. You'll note that we give exact temperature settings when the electric frypan is used.

In a few recipes, either the skillet or the electric frypan is preferred for best results, and we have indicated this. In addition, an electric wok can be used instead of a skillet or electric frypan in preparing any of the recipes in Chapter 2, "Easy Stir-Fried Dishes."

When we asked the home economists in our Farm Journal Test Kitchens for a few suggestions that you might use to streamline your meal preparation, they came up with four basic points.

First, read the recipe carefully to be sure that you have all the ingredients and equipment before you begin.

Next, gather together all the ingredients *before* you start cooking. You'll be amazed at how much time you've wasted before on unneeded trips from one end of your kitchen to the other.

Third, cut and/or measure all the ingredients. (We thought this was so important that we made it the first step in most of the skillet recipes in this book.)

Finally, follow directions carefully.

We enjoyed creating this collection of timesaving skillet specialties, and we hope you'll enjoy using it and sharing the results with your family and friends.

—Patricia A. Ward

1 30-minute specials

During the busy planting and harvesting seasons, farm and ranch women depend on recipes for nourishing dishes that can be prepared in a jiffy. As one Kansas woman put it, "We are farmers, and hurry-up meals count."

In this chapter, we've collected skillet recipes created by—and for—women who are just too busy to spend a lot of time in the kitchen. Whether you live on a wheat farm or in a city condominium, you'll find these recipes especially useful for hurried days. Each one can be prepared and cooked in 30 minutes or less.

Included in this chapter are such specialties as curried turkey flavored with apple, onion, mushrooms and sour cream; an easy No-Bake Lasagne featuring pork sausage, cottage cheese and noodles; a Hamburger Pie with a filling of ground beef and green beans ringed with cheesy mashed potatoes; and a skillet-baked pepperoni pizza topped with melted mozzarella cheese and a sprinkle of oregano.

All of these recipes reflect the flavor and the philosophy of traditional country cooking: For better economy, taste and nutrition, the emphasis is on fresh fruits and vegetables.

Each recipe is a complete meal in itself, or needs only a crisp green salad and fruit or dessert to round out the menu.

2/Easy hamburger stroganoff

- *Preparation time: 5 minutes*
- *Cooking time: 17 minutes*

This inexpensive version of stroganoff uses ground beef instead of sirloin steak. It's also delicious served over cooked rice.

1 lb. ground chuck
½ c. chopped onion
1 clove garlic, minced
1 tsp. beef bouillon
　granules
1 tsp. Worcestershire
　sauce
¼ tsp. paprika

⅛ tsp. pepper
1 (10¾-oz.) can condensed
　cream of mushroom
　soup
1 (4-oz.) can mushroom
　stems and pieces
1 c. dairy sour cream
12 slices bread, toasted

Cut and measure all ingredients before starting to cook.

Cook ground chuck, onion and garlic in 10″ skillet over medium-high heat 5 minutes or until browned. Drain off fat.

Stir in beef bouillon granules, Worcestershire sauce, paprika, pepper, mushroom soup and undrained mushrooms. Cook until mixture comes to a boil, about 1 minute.

Reduce heat to low and simmer 10 minutes, stirring occasionally.

Stir some of hot mixture into sour cream. Then stir sour cream mixture into skillet. Heat 1 minute more. (Do not boil.) Serve over toast.

Makes 6 servings.

3/Hearty tomato rice soup

- *Preparation time: 5 minutes*
- *Cooking time: 25 minutes*

This super-quick soup makes a perfect summer supper or lunch. To complete the meal, add a crisp green salad and crusty brown rolls.

1 lb. ground chuck
1 c. chopped onion
1 c. finely chopped celery
1 (28-oz.) can tomatoes, cut up
2½ c. water

⅓ c. uncooked regular rice
3 beef bouillon cubes
1 tsp. Worcestershire sauce
1 bay leaf
¼ tsp. pepper

Cut and measure all ingredients before starting to cook.

Cook ground chuck, onion and celery in 12″ skillet or electric frypan over medium heat (350°) 5 minutes or until browned. Pour off excess fat.

Stir in tomatoes, water, rice, bouillon cubes, Worcestershire sauce, bay leaf and pepper. Cook until mixture comes to a boil, about 2 minutes.

Reduce heat to low (220°). Cover and simmer 18 minutes or until rice is tender, stirring occasionally.

Makes 4 to 6 servings.

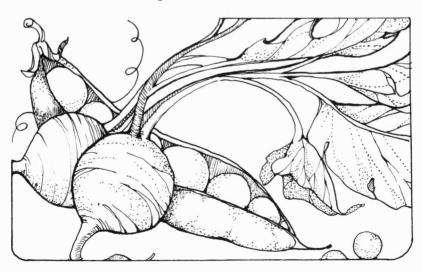

4/South-of-the-border pizza

• Preparation time: 9 minutes
• Cooking time: 21 minutes

We've topped a pizza crust with a beef filling, shredded lettuce and tomatoes. It looks and tastes like a giant-sized taco.

½ c. chopped onion
1 lb. ground beef
½ (13-oz.) pkg. pizza crust
   mix
⅔ c. very warm water
1 (15-oz.) can red kidney
   beans, drained
1 (8-oz.) can tomato sauce

4 drops Tabasco sauce
2 tsp. chili powder
½ tsp. salt
1 c. shredded Cheddar
   cheese
1½ c. shredded lettuce
1 c. chopped tomato
Taco sauce

Cut and measure onion.

Cook ground beef and onion in 12″ electric frypan over medium heat (350⁰) 4 minutes or until browned.

Meanwhile, combine pizza crust mix and warm water according to package directions. Cover and let rest in warm place 5 minutes.

While dough is resting, cut and measure remaining ingredients.

Remove meat mixture from skillet and place in bowl, draining off excess fat. Stir in kidney beans, tomato sauce, Tabasco sauce, chili powder and salt; set aside. Rinse out electric frypan.

Grease frypan with shortening. Spread dough with rubber spatula over bottom and 1″ up sides of same electric frypan. Spread meat mixture over dough to within ¾″ of edges.

Set heat at medium (350⁰). Cover, with vents open, and bake 10 minutes.

Uncover. Sprinkle with cheese. Bake, uncovered, 7 minutes more or until bottom of crust is browned. Slide out of skillet. Sprinkle with lettuce and tomato. Cut into 8 pieces. Serve with taco sauce.

Makes 8 servings.

5/Corn-stuffed burgers

- *Preparation time: 14 minutes*
- *Cooking time: 15 minutes*

These corn-stuffed beef burgers are served in a rich and velvety mushroom sauce. Delicious with rice or mashed potatoes.

1 (8-oz.) can whole kernel corn, drained
½ c. soft bread crumbs
¼ c. minced onion
2 tblsp. minced fresh parsley
½ c. shredded Cheddar cheese
1 egg, beaten

1 tsp.Worcestershire sauce
2 lb. ground chuck
1 tsp. salt
¼ tsp. pepper
1 egg, beaten
1 (10¾-oz.) can condensed golden mushroom soup
1 (8-oz.) can tomato sauce

Cut and measure all ingredients before starting to cook.

Combine corn, bread crumbs, onion, parsley, Cheddar cheese, 1 egg and Worcestershire sauce in bowl. Mix lightly, but well.

Combine ground chuck, salt, pepper and 1 egg in bowl. Mix lightly, but well. Shape mixture into 16 (4″) patties. Place a scant ¼ c. of the corn filling in center of 8 patties. Top each with another meat pattie. Seal edges and round up patties, making them 3½″ in diameter.

Preheat 12″ skillet or electric frypan over medium heat (350⁰) 3 minutes or until hot.

Cook stuffed beef patties 5 minutes. When browned, turn over and cook 5 minutes on other side. Remove from skillet and keep warm. Drain off fat and wipe out skillet with paper towel.

Combine mushroom soup and tomato sauce in same skillet. Place over medium heat (350⁰) 2 minutes or until hot. Spoon over beef patties.

Makes 8 servings.

6/Hamburger-potato skillet

• Preparation time: 5 minutes
• Cooking time: 25 minutes

Here's a 30-minute meal featuring ground beef with brown gravy, mixed vegetables and mashed potato mounds topped with cheese.

1½ lb. ground beef
½ c. chopped onion
½ c. chopped celery
1 tsp. Worcestershire
  sauce
1½ tsp. salt
¼ tsp. pepper
2 (¾-oz.) pkg. brown gravy
  mix

2 c. water
1 (10-oz.) pkg. frozen
  mixed vegetables (2 c.)
Instant mashed potatoes
  for 6 servings
½ c. shredded pasteurized
  process American
  cheese

Cut and measure all ingredients before starting to cook.

Cook ground beef, onion and celery in 12″ skillet or electric frypan over medium heat (350⁰) 10 minutes or until browned.

Add Worcestershire sauce, salt, pepper, brown gravy mix, water and mixed vegetables. Cook until mixture comes to a boil, about 2 minutes.

Reduce heat to low (220⁰). Cover and simmer 10 minutes or until vegetables are tender.

Meanwhile, prepare mashed potatoes according to package directions.

Drop mashed potatoes in 6 spoonfuls on meat mixture. Sprinkle potatoes with cheese. Cover and simmer 3 minutes more or until cheese is melted.

Makes 6 servings.

7/Western-style beans

- *Preparation time: 4 minutes*
- *Cooking time: 22 minutes*

A Nebraska farm woman says that her family likes this casserole because it's different from the usual meat-and-potato dish.

1 lb. ground chuck	**½ c. ketchup**
½ c. chopped onion	**1 tblsp. prepared mustard**
¼ c. chopped green pepper	**1 tsp. chili powder**
2 (16-oz.) cans pork and beans in tomato sauce	

Cut and measure all ingredients before starting to cook.

Cook ground chuck, onion and green pepper in 10″ skillet over medium-high heat 10 minutes or until well browned.

Stir in pork and beans, ketchup, mustard and chili powder. Cook until mixture comes to a boil, about 2 minutes.

Reduce heat to medium. Cover and simmer 10 minutes, stirring occasionally.

Makes 4 servings.

8/Beef with eggplant

• *Preparation time: 15 minutes*
• *Cooking time: 15 minutes*

This tasty version of eggplant Parmesan is rich in nutrients and cooks in just 15 minutes in your skillet.

1 lb. ground chuck
¼ c. chopped onion
¼ c. chopped green pepper
1 clove garlic, minced
1 tblsp. flour
1 (8-oz.) can tomato sauce
¾ c. water
½ tsp. salt
½ tsp. dried oregano leaves

½ tsp. chili powder
⅛ tsp. pepper
1 small unpared eggplant, cut into ½" slices (1 lb.)
1 c. shredded Cheddar cheese
2 tblsp. chopped fresh parsley

Cut and measure all ingredients before starting to cook.

Cook ground chuck, onion, green pepper and garlic in 12" skillet or electric frypan over medium heat (350⁰) 6 minutes or until browned.

Stir in flour, tomato sauce, water, salt, oregano, chili powder and pepper. Arrange eggplant slices on top.

Reduce heat to low (220⁰). Cover and simmer 7 minutes or until eggplant is tender.

Sprinkle with cheese. Cover and cook 2 minutes or until cheese is melted.

Sprinkle with parsley before serving.

Makes 4 servings.

9/Tacos

- *Preparation time: 5 minutes*
- *Cooking time: 24 minutes*

This is one sandwich that uses no bread. Just spoon the meat filling into a taco shell and top with cheese, lettuce and tomato.

⅓ c. chopped onion
1 clove garlic, minced
1 lb. ground chuck
2 tblsp. chili powder
1 tsp. salt
½ tsp. ground cumin
1 tsp. sugar
2 drops Tabasco sauce

1 c. water
2 tblsp. taco sauce
12 taco shells
1 c. shredded Cheddar cheese
1 c. shredded lettuce
1 large tomato, chopped

Cut and measure onion and garlic.

Cook ground chuck, onion and garlic in 10″ skillet over medium-high heat 8 minutes or until browned. Drain off excess fat.

Meanwhile, cut and measure remaining ingredients.

Add chili powder, salt, cumin, sugar, Tabasco sauce, water and taco sauce to skillet. Cook until mixture comes to a boil, about 1 minute.

Reduce heat to low. Simmer, uncovered, 15 minutes or just until liquid is reduced.

Spoon some of meat mixture into each taco shell. Top each with cheese, lettuce and tomato. Pass additional taco sauce, if you wish.

Makes 12 tacos or 6 servings.

10/Beef and noodle medley

- *Preparation time: 6 minutes*
- *Cooking time: 24 minutes*

A Montana ranch woman always keeps ingredients on hand for this recipe. She serves this fast-fix meal on extra-busy days.

1 lb. ground beef
1½ c. chopped celery
½ c. chopped onion
½ c. chopped green pepper
2 c. uncooked wide
  noodles
1 (16-oz.) can red kidney
  beans

1 (35-oz.) can Italian
  tomatoes, cut up
1 (4-oz.) can sliced
  mushrooms
2½ tsp. salt
¾ tsp. chili powder
¼ tsp. pepper

Cut and measure all ingredients before starting to cook.

Cook ground beef, celery, onion and green pepper in 10″ skillet over medium heat 8 minutes or until browned.

Stir in noodles, undrained kidney beans, tomatoes, undrained mushrooms, salt, chili powder and pepper. Cook until mixture comes to a boil, about 1 minute.

Reduce heat to low. Cover and simmer 15 minutes or until noodles are tender.

Makes 6 to 8 servings.

11/Rancher's beef stew

- *Preparation time: 10 minutes*
- *Cooking time: 20 minutes*

Ground beef is shaped into square patties in this recipe. After browning, they are cut into cubes for this family-style dish.

1 lb. ground chuck
½ c. soft bread crumbs
⅓ c. minced onion
2 tblsp. chopped fresh
  parsley
½ tsp. salt
½ tsp. dried thyme leaves
1 egg, slightly beaten
1 medium onion, sliced
Water
2 (10½-oz.) cans
  condensed beef broth

3 medium potatoes, pared
  and cut into 1″ cubes
  (1 lb.)
2 c. pared carrot strips,
  2″ lengths
1 (9-oz.) pkg. frozen cut
  green beans, thawed
  (2 c.)
3 tblsp. cornstarch
¼ c. water
1 tsp. browning for gravy

Cut and measure first 7 ingredients for meat patties.

Combine ground chuck, bread crumbs, ⅓ c. minced onion, parsley, salt, thyme and egg in bowl. Mix lightly, but well. Shape mixture into 4 (3″) square meat patties.

Cook meat patties in 12″ skillet or electric frypan over medium heat (350⁰) 3 minutes.

Meanwhile, slice onion and add enough water to beef broth to make 3 c. Turn patties over and add sliced onion to skillet. Cook 3 minutes more.

Meanwhile, cut and measure potatoes and carrots.

Remove patties from skillet. Add 3 c. liquid, potatoes, carrots and beans to skillet. Reduce heat to low (220⁰). Cover and simmer 8 minutes.

Meanwhile, cut each beef pattie into 6 cubes.

Add cubed meat to skillet. Cover and simmer 5 minutes more.

Combine cornstarch and ¼ c. water in bowl; stir to blend. Stir into hot mixture with browning for gravy. Cook, stirring constantly, until mixture boils and thickens, about 1 minute.

Makes 4 to 6 servings.

12/Spanish-style squash

• Preparation time: 7 minutes
• Cooking time: 23 minutes

This beef-zucchini skillet helps prove that the simplest foods are often the best. It's lightly seasoned with cumin and garlic salt.

1 lb. ground beef
⅓ c. chopped onion
1½ lb. zucchini, sliced
  (about 5 c.)
½ tsp. salt

¼ tsp. garlic salt
¼ tsp. ground cumin
⅛ tsp. pepper
1 (8-oz.) can tomato sauce
1 (12-oz.) can mexicorn

Cut and measure all ingredients before starting to cook.

Cook ground beef and onion in 10″ skillet over medium heat 8 minutes or until browned.

Add zucchini, salt, garlic salt, cumin and pepper. Cook 3 minutes.

Add tomato sauce and mexicorn. Cook until mixture comes to a boil, about 2 minutes.

Reduce heat to low. Cover and simmer 10 minutes or until squash is tender. Add a little water, if necessary.

Makes 6 servings.

13/Hamburger pie

- *Preparation time: 2 minutes*
- *Cooking time: 28 minutes*

Meat-and-potato lovers will like this green bean-beef mixture laced with tomato soup and topped with a ring of cheesy potatoes.

1 c. water
1 (10-oz.) pkg. frozen cut
    green beans
1 lb. ground chuck
1 c. chopped onion
1 clove garlic, minced
¼ tsp. salt
⅛ tsp. pepper
1 (10¾-oz.) can condensed
    tomato soup

⅓ c. water
Instant mashed potatoes
    for 8 servings
1 c. shredded Cheddar
    cheese
2 tblsp. chopped fresh
    parsley

Heat 1 c. water in 10″ skillet over high heat 2 minutes or until it comes to a boil. Add beans and return to a boil. Cover and cook 6 minutes or until tender. Drain in colander.

While beans are cooking, cut and measure remaining ingredients.

Wipe out skillet. Cook ground chuck, onion and garlic in same skillet over medium heat 10 minutes or until browned.

Stir in salt, pepper, tomato soup, water and green beans. Reduce heat to low. Cover and cook 5 minutes.

Meanwhile, prepare instant mashed potatoes according to package directions. Stir in cheese.

Drop potatoes in spoonfuls around edge of skillet, making two rings. Cover and cook 5 minutes more.

Sprinkle parsley over potatoes before serving.

Makes 4 servings.

14/Beef and bean burritos

- *Preparation time: 10 minutes*
- *Cooking time: 11 minutes*

This popular Southwestern recipe features warm tortillas wrapped around a beef and bean filling topped with cheese and sour cream.

1 (12½-oz.) pkg. flour
  tortillas (10)
1 (15-oz.) can red kidney
  beans
1 lb. ground chuck
½ c. chopped onion
1 clove garlic, minced
⅓ c. taco sauce
1 tblsp. chili powder

¾ tsp. salt
6 drops Tabasco sauce
¼ c. grated Parmesan
  cheese
1 c. shredded Cheddar
  cheese
¼ c. chopped onion
1 c. dairy sour cream

Cut and measure all ingredients before starting to cook.

Wrap flour tortillas in aluminum foil. Warm in 350⁰ oven, about 15 minutes.

Mash kidney beans in their liquid until smooth, using a fork.

Meanwhile, cook ground chuck, ½ c. chopped onion and garlic in 10″ skillet over medium heat 8 minutes or until well browned. Drain off excess fat.

Stir in mashed kidney beans, taco sauce, chili powder, salt, Tabasco sauce and Parmesan cheese. Heat 3 minutes.

Spoon approximately ⅓ c. meat filling down center of each flour tortilla. Top each with Cheddar cheese, onion and a little sour cream.

Fold up tortilla like an envelope, starting at the right side. Or tuck two sides over filling and roll up.

Makes 10 burritos.

15/Ground beef sizzle

- *Preparation time: 5 minutes*
- *Cooking time: 25 minutes*

A high-protein meal especially suited to a cold wintry evening. Add hot corn bread and creamy coleslaw to complete the menu.

2 lb. ground beef
1 c. thinly sliced onion
1 c. chopped green pepper
1 (16-oz.) can whole-kernel corn
1 (15½-oz.) can red kidney beans
2 (8-oz.) cans tomato sauce

1 tblsp. steak sauce
1 tsp. salt
1 tsp. dried marjoram leaves
¼ tsp. pepper
1 bay leaf

Cut and measure all ingredients before starting to cook.

Cook ground beef, onion and green pepper in 10″ skillet over medium heat 8 minutes or until browned.

Add undrained corn, undrained kidney beans, tomato sauce, steak sauce, salt, marjoram, pepper and bay leaf. Cook until mixture comes to a boil, about 2 minutes.

Reduce heat to low. Cover and simmer 15 minutes, adding water if necessary.

Makes 4 to 6 servings.

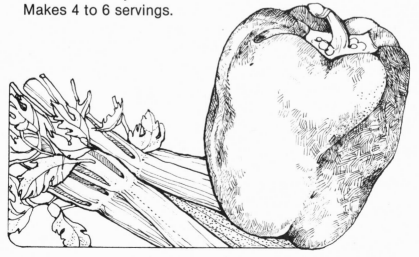

16/Summer zucchini with beef

• Preparation time: 8 minutes
• Cooking time: 22 minutes

Change the vegetables in this recipe to suit the season. It's also good made with shredded cabbage, sliced carrots and canned corn.

1 c. chopped onion
¾ c. chopped green pepper
1 clove garlic, minced
1 lb. ground beef
1½ tsp. salt
¼ tsp. pepper
1 tsp. chili powder
5 c. sliced, unpared zucchini or yellow summer squash

2 large tomatoes, peeled and chopped
1¼ c. fresh whole kernel corn, cut from the cob (about 3 medium cobs)
2 tblsp. chopped pimientos
¼ c. chopped fresh parsley

Cut and measure onion, green pepper and garlic.

Cook ground beef, onion, green pepper and garlic in 12″ skillet or electric frypan over medium heat (350⁰) 10 minutes or until browned.

Meanwhile, cut and measure remaining ingredients.

Stir in salt, pepper, chili powder, zucchini, tomatoes, corn, pimientos and parsley. Cook until mixture comes to a boil, about 2 minutes.

Reduce heat to low (220⁰). Cover and simmer 10 minutes or until vegetables are tender.

Makes 6 servings.

17/Ground beef pizza

- *Preparation time: 9 minutes*
- *Cooking time: 21 minutes*

A skillet pizza is just as delicious as a baked one—and you don't heat up your kitchen by turning on the oven.

½ lb. ground chuck
½ (13-oz.) pkg. pizza crust mix
⅔ c. very warm water
1 (8-oz.) can stewed tomatoes
⅓ c. chopped onion
1 clove garlic, minced
½ tsp. Italian herb seasoning

⅛ tsp. salt
1 c. shredded mozzarella cheese
¼ c. sliced pimiento-stuffed olives
⅓ c. grated Romano cheese

Cook ground beef in 12″ electric frypan over medium heat (350⁰) 4 minutes or until browned.

Meanwhile, combine pizza crust mix and warm water according to package directions. Cover and let rest in warm place 5 minutes.

While dough is resting, cut and measure remaining ingredients. Purée stewed tomatoes in blender until smooth; set aside.

Remove beef from skillet and place in bowl, draining off excess fat. Rinse out frypan.

Grease frypan with shortening. Spread dough with rubber spatula over bottom and 1″ up sides of electric frypan.

Combine puréed tomatoes, onion, garlic, Italian herb seasoning and salt in bowl; mix well.

Spread tomato mixture over dough. Top with ground beef, then mozzarella, sliced olives and then, sprinkle with Romano cheese.

Set heat at medium (350⁰). Cover, with vent open, and bake 10 minutes.

Uncover. Bake, uncovered, 7 minutes more or until crust is browned on bottom.

Slide pizza out of skillet and cut into squares.

Makes 8 servings.

18/Double cheese macaroni

- *Preparation time: 5 minutes*
- *Cooking time: 25 minutes*

An extra-creamy version of baked macaroni and cheese that's been adapted to skillet cookery. Ham and Swiss cheese make it different.

3 c. water
1 tsp. salt
1 c. uncooked elbow
  macaroni
¼ c. butter or regular
  margarine
1 tblsp. minced onion
1 tblsp. chopped fresh
  parsley
2 tblsp. flour
1½ c. milk

1 c. shredded Cheddar
  cheese
½ c. shredded Swiss
  cheese
½ c. slivered fully cooked
  ham
3 eggs, well beaten
¼ tsp. salt
⅛ tsp. pepper
Paprika

Heat water and 1 tsp. salt in 12″ skillet or electric frypan over medium heat (350⁰) 5 minutes or until it comes to a boil.

Meanwhile, cut or measure macaroni, butter, onion, parsley, flour and milk.

Add macaroni to boiling water and return to a boil. Reduce heat to low (240⁰). Cover and cook 10 minutes, stirring occasionally.

While macaroni is cooking, cut and measure remaining ingredients.

Drain macaroni in colander and rinse with cold water.

Melt butter in same skillet over low heat (240⁰), about 2 minutes. Add onion and parsley; sauté 1 minute. Stir in flour. Gradually stir in milk. Cook, stirring constantly, until mixture boils and thickens, about 4 minutes.

Add Cheddar cheese and Swiss cheese; stir until melted, about 1 minute. Add ham and macaroni. Turn off heat.

Stir some of the hot mixture into eggs. Then stir egg mixture back into skillet. Turn heat to low (220⁰) and stir for 2 minutes. Stir in ¼ tsp. salt and pepper. Sprinkle with paprika before serving.

Makes 4 to 6 servings.

19/Ham and cabbage soup

This nourishing and creamy cabbage soup is just right for extra-cold days. Welcome your family home with this easy meal.

6 c. shredded cabbage
1 (10-oz.) pkg. frozen
   whole-kernel corn (2½ c.)
1 lb. fully cooked ham, cut
   in 2 × ¼″ strips
2 c. chicken broth
1 tsp. sugar

¼ tsp. salt
⅛ tsp. pepper
2 tblsp. flour
1¾ c. milk
2 tblsp. chopped fresh
   parsley

Cut and measure all ingredients before starting to cook.

Combine cabbage, corn, ham, chicken broth, sugar, salt and pepper in 12″ skillet or electric frypan over medium heat (350⁰). Cook until mixture comes to a boil, about 2 minutes.

Reduce heat to low (220⁰). Cover and simmer 17 minutes or until cabbage is tender, stirring occasionally.

Combine flour and milk in jar. Cover and shake until blended. Stir into cabbage mixture. Cook over medium heat (350⁰), stirring constantly, until mixture boils and thickens, about 3 minutes.

Ladle into bowls and garnish with parsley.

Makes about 2 quarts.

20/Quick ham- macaroni skillet

• *Preparation time: 8 minutes*
• *Cooking time: 22 minutes*

Peas and tomatoes provide added nutrition to this easy version of a traditional favorite. (See photo, Plate 4.)

2 tblsp. cooking oil
1 c. chopped onion
3 c. water
8 oz. uncooked elbow
  macaroni
1 (10¾-oz.) can
  condensed cream of
  mushroom soup
¾ c. milk
1 tsp. dry mustard

1 lb. fully cooked ham
  steak, cut into 2 × ¼"
  strips
2 c. shredded Cheddar
  cheese
1 (10-oz.) pkg. frozen
  peas, thawed
10 cherry tomatoes,
  halved

Cut and measure all ingredients before starting to cook.

Heat oil in 12" skillet or electric frypan over medium heat (300⁰) 5 minutes or until hot.

Add onion and sauté 2 minutes. Increase heat to medium (350⁰). Add water. Cover and cook until it comes to a boil, about 2 minutes.

Add macaroni and return to a boil. Reduce heat to low (220⁰). Cover and cook 9 minutes, stirring occasionally, until water is absorbed.

Combine mushroom soup and milk in bowl; stir until blended. Stir in mustard.

Add soup mixture to macaroni. Then stir in ham, Cheddar cheese and peas. Cover and cook 4 minutes or until thoroughly heated, stirring frequently.

Serve garnished with cherry tomatoes.

Makes 6 to 8 servings.

21/Grilled ham salad sandwiches

- *Preparation time: 19 minutes*
- *Cooking time: 10 minutes*

These knife-and-fork sandwiches are spread with ham salad, dipped into an egg mixture and grilled to a golden brown color.

1 c. ground fully cooked
   ham
¼ c. finely chopped celery
1 tblsp. sweet pickle relish
1 tblsp. finely chopped
   onion
1 tblsp. chopped fresh
   parsley
¼ c. mayonnaise
8 slices pasteurized
   process American
   cheese

8 slices white bread
3 eggs, slightly beaten
¾ c. milk
½ tsp. salt
⅛ tsp. pepper
2 tblsp. butter or regular
   margarine

Cut and measure all ingredients before starting to cook.

Combine ham, celery, pickle relish, onion, parsley and mayonnaise in bowl. Mix well.

Place 1 slice of cheese on each of 4 slices bread. Spread ¼ c. ham mixture on top. Top each with 1 more slice cheese. Place a slice of bread on each.

Combine eggs, milk, salt and pepper in 9″ square baking pan. Beat with rotary beater until blended.

Dip sandwiches into egg-milk mixture, coating both sides well. Be sure to use all of egg mixture.

Melt butter in 12″ electric frypan over medium heat (320⁰), about 2 minutes. Brown sandwiches on one side, about 4 minutes. Turn sandwiches over carefully. Cook on other side 4 minutes or until browned.

Makes 4 servings.

Note: A round 12″ skillet can be used, but only 2 sandwiches fit at a time. (Total cooking time: 18 minutes.)

22/Curried chicken skillet

• *Preparation time: none*
• *Cooking time: 30 minutes*

Here's a company recipe for days when your schedule keeps you out of the kitchen. (See photo, Plate 3.)

¼ c. cooking oil
3 whole chicken breasts, split (about 3 lb.)
¾ tsp. salt
½ c. chopped onion
1 clove garlic, minced
1 c. green pepper strips
¼ lb. fresh mushrooms, sliced

Water
2 (10½-oz.) cans condensed chicken broth
1½ c. uncooked regular rice
1 tsp. curry powder
¼ tsp. salt
1 (6-oz.) pkg. frozen pea pods, thawed

Heat oil in 12″ skillet or electric frypan over high heat (400⁰) 2 minutes.

Season chicken with ¾ tsp. salt. Brown chicken on all sides in hot oil, about 7 minutes.

Meanwhile, cut and measure remaining ingredients.

Push chicken to one side of skillet. Add onion, garlic, green pepper strips and mushrooms. Sauté 3 minutes.

Add enough water to chicken broth to make 3¼ c. Stir 3¼ c. liquid, rice, curry powder and ¼ tsp. salt into skillet. Rearrange chicken on top of rice mixture. Cook until mixture comes to a boil, about 2 minutes.

Reduce heat to low (220⁰). Cover and simmer 14 minutes, stirring occasionally.

Add pea pods. Cover and simmer 2 minutes more. Serve immediately.

Makes 6 servings.

23/Chicken and rice

• *Preparation time: 3 minutes*
• *Cooking time: 27 minutes*

Plan to serve this skillet meal when you really don't have time to cook. It's easy to assemble and cooks in only 27 minutes.

1 c. chopped celery	⅛ tsp. powdered saffron
½ c. chopped onion	1 c. uncooked regular rice
½ c. butter or regular margarine	1½ c. diced pared carrots
Water	½ tsp. salt
2 (10¾-oz.) cans condensed chicken broth	⅛ tsp. pepper
	3 c. cubed cooked chicken
	¼ c. chopped fresh parsley

Cut and measure celery and onion.

Melt butter in 12″ skillet or electric frypan over medium heat (300⁰), about 2 minutes.

Meanwhile, add enough water to chicken broth to make 3½ c.; set aside.

Add celery and onion to skillet. Sauté 5 minutes or until tender.

While vegetables are sautéing, cut and measure saffron, rice, carrots, salt and pepper.

Add 3½ c. chicken broth mixture, saffron, rice, carrots, salt and pepper to skillet. Bring mixture to a boil, about 1 minute.

Reduce heat to low (220⁰). Cover and simmer 15 minutes.

Meanwhile, cut and measure chicken and parsley.

Add chicken and parsley. Cover and simmer 4 minutes more or until rice is tender.

Makes 6 servings.

24/Spicy chicken livers

• Preparation time: 10 minutes
• Cooking time: 20 minutes

This iron-rich main dish tastes as good as it looks! It's been a favorite in a North Dakota farm family for more than 50 years.

2 tblsp. cooking oil
2 c. sliced onion
1½ c. green pepper strips
1 lb. chicken livers

1 large tomato, peeled and
    cut into 16 wedges
½ tsp. salt
⅛ tsp. pepper

Cut and measure all ingredients before starting to cook.

Heat oil in 12″ skillet or electric frypan over medium heat (300⁰) 5 minutes or until hot.

Add onion and green pepper to hot oil. Sauté 10 minutes or until tender.

Add chicken livers, tomato, salt and pepper. Cook 5 minutes, turning chicken livers frequently, or until browned.

Makes 4 to 6 servings.

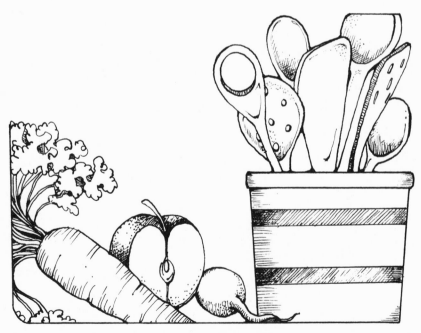

25/Monte Cristo sandwiches

- *Preparation time: 9 minutes*
- *Cooking time: 10 minutes*

These unique brunch or supper sandwiches are dipped into an egg mixture before grilling and served with a delicate mustard sauce.

8 slices pasteurized
   process American
   cheese
8 slices white bread
4 oz. sliced turkey breast
4 oz. sliced boiled ham
3 eggs
¾ c. milk
½ tsp. salt

⅛ tsp. pepper
2 tblsp. butter or regular
   margarine
¾ c. dairy sour cream
½ c. milk
4 tsp. prepared yellow
   mustard
¼ tsp. prepared
   horseradish

Cut and measure all ingredients before starting to cook.

Place 1 slice of cheese on each of 4 slices bread. Top with one fourth of the turkey and one fourth of the ham. Top each with 1 more slice cheese. Place a slice of bread on each.

Combine eggs, ¾ c. milk, salt and pepper in 9″ square baking pan. Beat until smooth, using a rotary beater. Dip sandwiches into egg-milk mixture, coating both sides well. Be sure to use all of egg mixture.

Melt butter in 12″ electric skillet over medium heat (320⁰), about 2 minutes.

Grill sandwiches in melted butter 4 minutes or until browned on bottom. Turn over carefully. Cook on other side, about 4 minutes.

Meanwhile, combine sour cream, ½ c. milk, mustard and horseradish in small bowl; mix well.

Serve sandwiches with sour cream sauce.

Makes 4 sandwiches.

Note: A round 12″ skillet can be used, but only 2 sandwiches will fit at one time. (Total cooking time: 18 minutes.)

26/Curried turkey with rice

Chicken can be substituted for turkey in this curried dish. Sour cream has been added to make the sauce extra-smooth.

¼ c. butter or regular margarine
1 c. sliced onion
1 medium apple, pared, cored and diced
¼ c. bias-cut pared carrots
¼ c. bias-cut celery
1 clove garlic, minced
⅓ c. flour
2 tblsp. curry powder
¼ tsp. ground ginger
¼ tsp. ground mace
⅛ tsp. pepper

2 c. chicken broth
1 (4-oz.) can sliced mushrooms
3 c. cubed cooked turkey
2 c. dairy sour cream
Hot cooked rice
Condiments: chopped onion, raisins, chopped green pepper, chopped hard-cooked egg, chopped peanuts and coconut

Cut and measure all ingredients before starting to cook.

Melt butter in 12″ skillet or electric frypan over medium heat (300⁰), about 2 minutes.

Add onion, apple, carrots, celery and garlic. Sauté 4 minutes or until apple is tender.

Combine flour, curry powder, ginger, mace and pepper. Slowly stir flour mixture into skillet. Gradually add chicken broth and undrained mushrooms. Cook, stirring constantly, until mixture comes to a boil, about 2 minutes.

Reduce heat to low (220⁰). Simmer, uncovered, 5 minutes.

Stir in turkey and heat 2 minutes. Stir a little of the hot mixture into sour cream. Then stir sour cream mixture into skillet and heat 2 minutes more. (Do not boil.) Serve with rice and pass a selection of condiments.

Makes 6 servings.

27/Cheesy creamed shrimp

• *Preparation time: 8 minutes*
• *Cooking time: 16 minutes*

Frozen cooked shrimp and canned potato soup make quick work of this supper dish. It's good ladled over toast points or fluffy rice.

2 tblsp. butter or regular margarine
¾ c. chopped green pepper
¾ c. chopped onion
2 tblsp. chopped fresh parsley
2 (10¾-oz.) cans condensed cream of potato soup
1 c. light cream
½ c. milk

1 tsp. Worcestershire sauce
¼ tsp. dry mustard
⅛ tsp. pepper
6 slices pasteurized process yellow American cheese, cut up
1 (6-oz.) pkg. frozen small cooked shrimp, thawed
Hot cooked rice
Paprika

Cut and measure all ingredients before starting to cook.

Melt butter in 10″ skillet over medium heat, about 2 minutes.

Add green pepper and onion. Saute 7 minutes or until tender.

Stir in parsley, potato soup, light cream, milk, Worcestershire sauce, mustard and pepper. Cook until mixture comes to a boil, about 3 minutes.

Reduce heat to low. Add cheese, stirring until melted, about 2 minutes. Add shrimp and heat 2 minutes.

Serve creamed shrimp on hot rice. Sprinkle with paprika before serving.

Makes 4 servings.

28/Tuna casserole with almonds

- *Preparation time: 4 minutes*
- *Cooking time: 26 minutes*

Your family can enjoy a tuna-rice casserole on a hot summer's day without heating up the kitchen if you use this skillet version.

1 c. uncooked regular rice
1 (10½-oz.) can condensed
  cream of celery soup
1 c. milk
1½ c. water
½ c. chopped onion
2 chicken bouillon cubes,
  crumbled
¼ tsp. Worcestershire
  sauce

¼ tsp. dry mustard
⅛ tsp. pepper
2 (7-oz.) cans chunk-style
  tuna, drained
1 (10-oz.) pkg. frozen peas,
  thawed
1 (3-oz.) can sliced
  mushrooms, drained
¼ c. toasted slivered
  almonds

Cut and measure all ingredients before starting to cook.

Combine rice, celery soup, milk, water, onion, chicken bouillon cubes, Worcestershire sauce, mustard and pepper in 12″ skillet or electric frypan; mix well. Cook over medium heat (350°), stirring occasionally, until mixture comes to a boil, about 2 minutes.

Reduce heat to low (220°). Cover and simmer 20 minutes or until rice is tender.

Stir in tuna, peas and mushrooms. Cover and heat 4 minutes, stirring occasionally.

Garnish with toasted slivered almonds before serving.

Makes 6 servings.

29/Grilled tuna sandwiches

- *Preparation time: 14 minutes*
- *Cooking time: 11 minutes*

Take advantage of bargain-priced chunk-style tuna and keep it handy for these sandwiches combining tuna salad with cheese.

1 (7-oz.) can chunk-style
  tuna, drained
½ c. finely chopped celery
2 tblsp. finely chopped
  onion
⅓ c. mayonnaise
8 slices whole wheat
  bread

8 slices pasteurized
  process American
  cheese
1 tomato, sliced
4 tblsp. soft butter or
  regular margarine

Cut and measure all ingredients before starting to cook.

Combine tuna, celery, onion and mayonnaise in bowl. Mix well.

Divide tuna mixture evenly among 4 slices of bread and spread in an even layer. Top tuna with 2 slices of the cheese. Arrange tomato slices on top. Place remaining bread slices on top.

Spread top side of sandwiches with soft butter, using one half of the butter.

Heat 12″ electric frypan over medium-high heat (380⁰) 5 minutes or until hot.

Place sandwiches buttered side down in frypan. Spread remaining butter on top of sandwiches. Cook 3 minutes or until browned. Turn over carefully. Cook 3 minutes more or until golden brown and cheese is melted.

Makes 4 servings.

Note: A round 12″ skillet can be used, but only 2 sandwiches will fit at one time. (Total cooking time: 17 minutes.)

*30/*Italian-style zucchini

• *Preparation time: 4 minutes*
• *Cooking time: 26 minutes*

All that's needed to complete this meal is a loaf of French bread, a crispy spinach salad and refreshing lemon or lime sherbet.

1 c. chopped onion
1 green pepper, cut into
  strips
1 clove garlic, minced
1 lb. bulk pork sausage
1 (16-oz.) can tomatoes,
  cut up
1 (8-oz.) can tomato sauce
1¼ tsp. salt

1 tsp. dried oregano leaves
¼ tsp. cayenne pepper
1¼ lb. zucchini, cut into
  ¼″ slices
1 c. uncooked wide
  noodles
1 c. water
1 c. shredded Cheddar
  cheese

Cut and measure onion, green pepper and garlic.

Cook pork sausage, onion, green pepper and garlic in 12″ skillet or electric frypan over medium heat (350⁰) 8 minutes or until browned.

Meanwhile, cut and measure remaining ingredients.

Stir tomatoes, tomato sauce, salt, oregano, cayenne pepper, zucchini, noodles and water into skillet. Cook until mixture comes to a boil, about 2 minutes.

Reduce heat to low (220⁰). Cover and simmer 15 minutes.

Sprinkle with cheese. Cover and cook 1 minute or until cheese melts.

Makes 6 servings.

31/Sausage macaroni dinner

- *Preparation time: 2 minutes*
- *Cooking time: 28 minutes*

"I served this dish often to my children when they were teenagers," wrote an Illinois mother. "It was one of their favorites."

1 lb. bulk pork sausage,
  cut into ½" slices
1 (16-oz.) can tomatoes,
  cut up
Water
3 tblsp. cooking oil
1 c. chopped green pepper

1 c. chopped onion
1 (7¼-oz.) pkg. macaroni
  and cheese dinner mix
¼ c. butter or regular
  margarine
½ c. milk

Cook sausage in 12" skillet or electric frypan over medium heat (300⁰) 12 minutes or until done, turning once. Remove and drain on paper towels. Wash out skillet.

While sausage is cooking, cut and measure remaining ingredients. Drain tomatoes, reserving juice. Add enough water to tomato juice to make 2¼ cups. Set aside.

Heat oil in same skillet over medium heat (350⁰) 1 minute. Add green pepper and onion. Sauté 2 minutes.

Stir in tomatoes and 2¼ c. tomato liquid. Cover and cook until mixture comes to a boil, about 1 minute. Stir in macaroni from dinner mix. Reduce heat to low (220⁰). Cover and simmer 10 minutes, stirring occasionally, until macaroni is tender and liquid is absorbed.

Stir in butter, milk and cheese sauce mix from dinner. Add sausage patties and heat 2 minutes.

Makes 4 servings.

32/No-bake lasagne

• *Preparation time: 5 minutes*
• *Cooking time: 25 minutes*

We've adapted this Italian favorite to easy skillet cookery and as a result reduced the total cooking time to less than 30 minutes.

1 (28-oz.) can Italian
   tomatoes
1 (6-oz.) can tomato paste
2 tblsp. chopped fresh
   parsley
1 tsp. dried oregano leaves
½ tsp. dried basil leaves
1 lb. bulk pork sausage
½ c. chopped onion
1 clove garlic, minced

1 (1½-oz.) pkg. spaghetti
   sauce mix
1 (1-lb.) carton creamed
   large-curd cottage
   cheese
4 c. uncooked medium
   noodles
8 oz. mozzarella cheese,
   shredded

Cut and measure first 8 ingredients.

Purée tomatoes with tomato paste in blender until smooth. Stir in parsley, oregano and basil; set aside.

Cook pork sausage, onion and garlic in 12″ skillet or electric frypan over medium heat (350⁰) 8 minutes or until well browned.

Meanwhile, cut and measure remaining ingredients.

Pour off excess fat from skillet. Stir one half of the spaghetti sauce mix into sausage mixture. Spoon cottage cheese evenly over sausage mixture. Arrange noodles on top.

Sprinkle with remaining spaghetti sauce mix. Pour tomato mixture evenly over noodles. Press down gently with spoon to moisten noodles.

Reduce heat to low (220⁰). Cover and simmer 15 minutes or until noodles are tender.

Sprinkle with mozzarella cheese. Cover and simmer 2 minutes more or until cheese melts.

Makes 8 servings.

33/Eggplant stacks with spaghetti sauce

• Preparation time: 8 minutes
• Cooking time: 22 minutes

You can add a special touch and more cheese flavor to this Italian-inspired dish by using freshly grated Parmesan or Romano cheese.

½ c. cooking oil
1 (1¼ lb.) eggplant, cut into 16 (⅜″) slices
1 (15½-oz.) jar spaghetti sauce with meat
4 oz. sliced Genoa hard salami

4 hard-cooked eggs, sliced
8 oz. mozzarella cheese, sliced
½ c. grated Parmesan cheese
½ tsp. dried oregano leaves

Cut and measure all ingredients before starting to cook.

Heat ¼ c. of the oil in 12″ skillet or electric frypan over medium heat (350⁰) 2 minutes or until hot.

Fry one half of the eggplant in hot oil 2 minutes. Turn over and fry 2 minutes more. Remove from skillet. Heat remaining oil in skillet 2 minutes or until hot. Repeat with remaining eggplant, about 4 minutes. Remove from skillet.

Turn off heat. Spread ½ c. of the spaghetti sauce in bottom of same skillet.

Make eggplant stacks by placing 8 eggplant slices in spaghetti sauce. Top each eggplant slice with salami, egg slice and mozzarella cheese. Sprinkle half of Parmesan cheese over stacks. Complete stacks by topping each with an eggplant slice, salami, egg slice and mozzarella cheese.

Pour remaining spaghetti sauce over all. Sprinkle with oregano. Cover and cook over low heat (200⁰) 10 minutes or until eggplant is tender.

Before serving, spoon some of the spaghetti sauce over stacks and sprinkle with remaining Parmesan cheese.

Makes 4 servings.

34/Pepperoni cheese pizza

* *Preparation time: 10 minutes*
* *Cooking time: 17 minutes*

If you can't find pizza crust mix in your local grocery store, use the homemade crust recipe given on page 157. (See photo, Plate 6.)

½ (13-oz.) pkg. pizza crust mix
⅔ c. very warm water
1 (8-oz.) can tomato sauce
½ tsp. dried oregano leaves
¼ c. chopped onion
1 c. shredded mozzarella cheese

2 oz. pepperoni, thinly sliced
1 (3-oz.) can sliced mushrooms, drained
½ c. green pepper strips
⅓ c. grated Parmesan cheese
½ tsp. dried oregano leaves

Cut and measure all ingredients before starting to cook.

Combine pizza crust mix and warm water according to package directions. Cover and let rest in warm place 5 minutes.

While dough is resting, grease 12″ electric frypan with shortening.

Spread dough with rubber spatula over bottom and 1″ up sides of greased electric frypan. Combine tomato sauce and ½ tsp. oregano. Spread tomato mixture over pizza dough. Top with onion, mozzarella cheese, pepperoni, mushrooms and green pepper strips. Then, sprinkle with Parmesan cheese and ½ tsp. oregano.

Set heat to medium (350⁰). Cover, with vents open, and bake 10 minutes.

Uncover. Bake, uncovered, 7 minutes more or until crust is browned on bottom.

Slide pizza out of skillet onto cutting board. Cut into squares.

Makes 8 servings.

35/Quick bean supper

• Preparation time: 7 minutes
• Cooking time: 20 minutes

Ordinary pork and beans look special when garnished with orange slices. Serve this hearty dish after an active day outdoors.

1 large orange
8 whole cloves
1 tblsp. butter or regular margarine
1 (12-oz.) can pork luncheon meat, cut into 8 lengthwise slices
2 tsp. prepared yellow mustard
¼ c. chopped onion

1 clove garlic, minced
2 (16-oz.) cans pork and beans in tomato sauce
2 tblsp. ketchup
1 tblsp. prepared yellow mustard
1 tblsp. brown sugar, packed
1 tsp. prepared horseradish

Cut and measure all ingredients before starting to cook.

Remove peel from orange, using a sharp knife. Be sure to remove all of white membrane. Cut orange into 4 thick slices. Cut each slice in half and place a clove in the center of each.

Melt butter in 10″ skillet over medium heat, about 1 minute.

Brown pork luncheon meat on both sides in hot butter, about 4 minutes. Remove from skillet and spread meat slices with 2 tsp. mustard.

Add onion and garlic to pan drippings. Sauté over medium-high heat 3 minutes or until tender.

Stir in pork and beans, ketchup, 1 tblsp. mustard, brown sugar and horseradish. Cook until mixture comes to a boil, about 2 minutes.

Reduce heat to low. Arrange meat slices, mustard side up, alternately with orange slices in a circle on top of bean mixture. Cover and simmer 10 minutes.

Makes 4 servings.

36/Easy barbecue buns

• *Preparation time: 8 minutes*
• *Cooking time: 22 minutes*

"My family loves spicy barbecue-flavored foods and this one is ready in a jiffy," a West Virginia woman wrote to us recently.

2 tblsp. butter or regular
  margarine
½ c. chopped onion
¼ c. chopped green
  pepper
1 (8-oz.) can tomato sauce
¼ c. water
¼ c. brown sugar, packed
3 tblsp. vinegar
2 tblsp. lemon juice
1 tsp. Worcestershire
  sauce

½ tsp. dry mustard
⅛ tsp. pepper
⅛ tsp. garlic powder
3 drops Tabasco sauce
1 (12-oz.) can pork
  luncheon meat, cut in
  2" strips
6 hamburger buns, split
  and toasted

Cut and measure all ingredients before starting to cook.

Melt butter in 10" skillet over medium-high heat about 1 minute.

Add onion and green pepper. Sauté 5 minutes or until tender. Stir in tomato sauce, water, brown sugar, vinegar, lemon juice, Worcestershire sauce, mustard, pepper, garlic powder, Tabasco sauce and luncheon meat. Cook until mixture comes to a boil, about 1 minute.

Reduce heat to low. Simmer, uncovered, 15 minutes.

Serve on toasted hamburger buns.

Makes 6 servings.

37/Speedy sauerkraut supper

• Preparation time: 5 minutes
• Cooking time: 22 minutes

When you need a hot meal in a hurry, try this recipe. Even though it's only cooked 22 minutes, the flavors blend beautifully.

1 large apple
1 tblsp. brown sugar, packed
2 tblsp. butter or regular margarine
1 (12-oz.) can pork luncheon meat, sliced

2 (16-oz.) cans sauerkraut, drained
¼ c. finely chopped onion
3 tblsp. brown sugar, packed
2 tblsp. cider vinegar

Core and pare apple. Cut into 4 rings. Sprinkle with 1 tblsp. brown sugar.

Melt butter in 10″ skillet over medium heat, about 2 minutes.

Add apple rings to skillet. Sauté apple rings in butter 10 minutes or until tender, turning as necessary.

Meanwhile, cut and measure remaining ingredients.

Remove apple rings from skillet. Add pork luncheon meat, sauerkraut, onion, 3 tblsp. brown sugar and vinegar to skillet. Top with apple rings.

Reduce heat to low. Cover and simmer 10 minutes or until thoroughly heated.

Makes 4 servings.

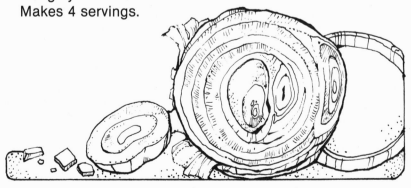

38/Easy macaroni skillet

- *Preparation time: 7 minutes*
- *Cooking time: 23 minutes*

Cottage cheese and Cheddar team up to make this macaroni dish slightly different. Mustard and horseradish add zip.

¼ c. butter or regular
  margarine
¼ c. flour
3 c. milk
2 tblsp. prepared yellow
  mustard
1 tblsp. prepared
  horseradish
4 c. cooked elbow
  macaroni

1 (12-oz.) can pork
  luncheon meat, cut into
  ¾" cubes
1 c. creamed large-curd
  cottage cheese
1 c. shredded Cheddar
  cheese
¼ c. chopped fresh parsley

Cut and measure all ingredients before starting to cook.

Melt butter in 12" skillet or electric frypan over medium heat (350⁰), about 2 minutes.

Stir in flour. Gradually stir in milk. Cook, stirring constantly, until mixture boils and thickens, about 10 minutes.

Stir in mustard, horseradish, cooked macaroni, pork luncheon meat, cottage cheese and Cheddar cheese. Cook until mixture comes to a boil, about 1 minute.

Reduce heat to low (220⁰). Cover and simmer 10 minutes. Sprinkle with parsley before serving.

Makes 6 servings.

39/Reuben sandwiches

• *Preparation time: 8 minutes*
• *Cooking time: 11 minutes*

Make this restaurant favorite at home. Each man-sized toasted sandwich is heaped with corned beef, sauerkraut and Swiss.

6 oz. thinly sliced corned beef
8 slices rye bread
1 (8-oz.) can sauerkraut, well drained

6 oz. thinly sliced Swiss cheese
4 tblsp. Russian dressing
3 tblsp. soft butter or regular margarine

Cut and measure all ingredients before starting to cook.

Divide corned beef evenly among 4 slices rye bread. Top each with one fourth of the sauerkraut. Evenly divide Swiss cheese among 4 sandwiches.

Spread 4 slices of bread with Russian dressing. Place bread, dressing side down, making 4 sandwiches. Generously butter top side of each sandwich, using about 1 tsp. butter on each.

Heat 12″ electric frypan to medium heat (320º), about 5 minutes.

Place sandwiches in hot frypan buttered side down. Butter top side of sandwich. Cook 3 minutes.

Turn sandwiches over carefully. Cook 3 minutes more or until bottom side is toasted and cheese is melted.

Makes 4 servings.

Note: A round 12″ skillet can be used, but only 2 sandwiches will fit in at a time. (Total cooking time: 17 minutes.)

40/Corned beef with cabbage

- *Preparation time: 8 minutes*
- *Cooking time: 22 minutes*

This New England boiled dinner takes only 30 minutes because it uses canned beef and potatoes as well as shredded cabbage.

1 (12-oz.) can corned beef, cut up
½ c. soft bread crumbs
1 egg
¼ c. mayonnaise
2 tblsp. butter or regular margarine
2 c. pared carrot strips, 2″ lengths
½ tsp. salt
⅛ tsp. pepper
1 (13¾-oz.) can chicken broth
6 c. shredded cabbage
2 (16-oz.) cans whole potatoes, drained

Cut and measure all ingredients except cabbage and potatoes before starting to cook.

Combine corned beef, bread crumbs, egg and mayonnaise in bowl. Mix lightly, but well. Shape mixture into 6 patties.

Melt butter in 12″ skillet or electric frypan over medium heat (300⁰), about 2 minutes.

Cook patties 5 minutes or until browned on both sides, turning once. Remove patties from skillet.

Add carrots, salt, pepper and chicken broth to skillet. Cook over low heat (220⁰) 5 minutes.

Meanwhile, shred cabbage and drain potatoes.

Stir in cabbage and potatoes. Arrange corned beef patties on top. Cover and cook over low heat (220⁰) 10 minutes or until cabbage is tender.

Makes 6 servings.

41/Beans and franks

• *Preparation time: 1 minute*
• *Cooking time: 29 minutes*

When the incomplete vegetable protein of beans is bolstered by the meat protein of frankfurters, the result is nutritious and flavorful.

½ c. water
¼ tsp. salt
1 (10-oz.) pkg. frozen Fordhook lima beans
1 (17-oz.) can red kidney beans, drained
1 (16-oz.) can pork and beans in tomato sauce
½ c. bottled barbecue sauce

⅓ c. minced onion
2 tblsp. brown sugar, packed
1 tblsp. prepared mustard
1 tsp. Worcestershire sauce
1 lb. frankfurters, cut into 1″ pieces

Heat water and salt in 10″ skillet over high heat 2 minutes or until it comes to a boil. Add lima beans and return to a boil, about 1 minute.

Reduce heat to low. Cover and simmer 14 minutes or until tender.

While beans are cooking, cut and measure remaining ingredients.

Drain lima beans. Add kidney beans, pork and beans, barbecue sauce, onion, brown sugar, mustard and Worcestershire sauce. Cook over medium-high heat 2 minutes or until mixture comes to a boil.

Reduce heat to low. Cover and simmer 5 minutes.

Add frankfurters. Cover and simmer 5 minutes more or until thoroughly heated, stirring occasionally.

Makes 6 servings.

42/Noodle frank skillet

This protein-packed frank dish is sauced with cottage cheese, tomato sauce and sour cream. (See photo, Plate 8.)

2 tblsp. cooking oil
½ c. sliced green onions
  and tops
1 clove garlic, minced
3 c. water
1 tsp. salt
8 oz. uncooked wide
  noodles
1 c. creamed large-curd
  cottage cheese

1 c. dairy sour cream
1 (8-oz.) can tomato
  sauce
1 lb. frankfurters
1 c. shredded Cheddar
  cheese
¼ c. chopped fresh
  parsley

Cut and measure all ingredients before starting to cook.

Heat oil in 12″ skillet or electric frypan over medium heat (350⁰) 5 minutes.

Add green onions and garlic; sauté 2 minutes.

Add water and salt. Cover and bring to a boil, about 3 minutes.

Add noodles. Cover and cook 10 minutes or until tender. Pour off excess water, if any.

Meanwhile, combine cottage cheese, sour cream and tomato sauce in bowl; mix well. Cut frankfurters in half lengthwise, cutting almost through. Stuff with Cheddar cheese.

Stir cottage cheese mixture into noodles. Arrange stuffed frankfurters on top, pinwheel fashion.

Reduce heat to low (220⁰). Cover and simmer 5 minutes, stirring occasionally, or until cheese melts. Garnish with parsley before serving.

Makes 6 servings.

43/Hot dogs with potatoes

- *Preparation time: 12 minutes*
- *Cooking time: 16 minutes*

A well-seasoned combo that's perfect for summer evenings. Round out the menu with sliced tomatoes and marinated cucumbers.

1 (6-oz.) pkg. hash brown potato mix
1 chicken bouillon cube
1½ c. boiling water
3 tblsp. butter or regular margarine
½ c. chopped onion
½ c. chopped green pepper
½ c. chopped celery

¼ c. chopped fresh parsley
2 c. creamed large-curd cottage cheese
1 c. dairy sour cream
1 lb. frankfurters, cut into 1″ slices
⅛ tsp. pepper
¼ c. sliced green onions

Combine hash brown potato mix, chicken bouillon cube and boiling water in bowl; mix well. Let stand 10 minutes.

Meanwhile, cut and measure remaining ingredients.

Melt butter in 12″ skillet or electric frypan over medium heat (350°), about 2 minutes.

Add onion, green pepper and celery to skillet. Sauté 4 minutes or until tender.

Stir in potato mixture, parsley, cottage cheese, sour cream, frankfurters and pepper.

Reduce heat to low (220°). Cover and simmer 10 minutes or until thoroughly heated. Garnish with sliced green onions.

Makes 6 servings.

44/Quick bean soup

- *Preparation time: 5 minutes*
- *Cooking time: 17 minutes*

No one will guess that this extra-flavorful bean soup took less than 20 minutes to cook. Sliced franks add both flavor and protein.

2 tblsp. cooking oil
1 c. chopped onion
½ c. chopped green pepper
2 (16-oz.) cans pork and
   beans in tomato sauce
1 (16-oz.) can tomatoes,
   cut up

1 (10½-oz.) can condensed
   beef broth
1 tblsp. prepared mustard
1 lb. frankfurters, bias-cut
   in ½″ pieces

Cut and measure all ingredients before starting to cook.

Heat oil in 12″ skillet or electric frypan over medium heat (350⁰) 5 minutes or until hot.

Add onion and green pepper. Sauté 5 minutes or until tender.

Stir in pork and beans, tomatoes, beef broth, mustard and frankfurters. Cook until mixture comes to a boil, about 2 minutes.

Reduce heat to low (220⁰). Simmer, uncovered, 5 minutes. Makes 9 cups.

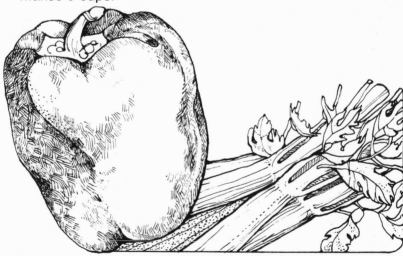

45/Barbecued beans with franks

- *Preparation time: 2 minutes*
- *Cooking time: 27 minutes*

Another popular version of franks and beans in a spicy barbecue-style sauce, this one flavored with Worcestershire and mustard.

2 c. water
1 (10-oz.) pkg. frozen
  Fordhook lima beans
1 (15-oz.) can red kidney
  beans, drained
1 (16-oz.) can pork and
  beans in tomato sauce
2 tblsp. brown sugar,
  packed

1 tsp. Worcestershire
  sauce
⅓ c. chopped green pepper
¼ c. finely chopped onion
⅓ c. ketchup
2 tblsp. cider vinegar
2 tsp. prepared mustard
1 lb. frankfurters

Heat water in 12″ skillet or electric frypan over high heat (420⁰) 2 minutes or until it comes to a boil.

Add lima beans and return to a boil. Reduce heat to low (220⁰). Cover and cook 15 minutes or until beans are tender.

Meanwhile, cut and measure remaining ingredients.

Drain lima beans in colander. Return to skillet. Add kidney beans, pork and beans, brown sugar, Worcestershire sauce, green pepper, onion, ketchup, vinegar, mustard and frankfurters.

Cover and cook over low heat (220⁰) 10 minutes or until thoroughly heated.

Makes 4 to 6 servings.

46/Western sandwiches

- *Preparation time: 7 minutes*
- *Cooking time: 17 minutes*

Makes enough mini-omelets for four. Each one is seasoned with green pepper, ham and onion and spiked with steak sauce.

2 tblsp. butter or regular margarine	3 tblsp. chopped onion
½ c. chopped fully cooked ham	4 eggs, beaten
	⅛ tsp. pepper
3 tblsp. chopped green pepper	⅛ tsp. steak sauce
	8 slices bread, toasted and buttered

Cut and measure all ingredients before starting to cook.

Melt butter in 10″ skillet over medium-high heat 1 minute. Add ham, green pepper and onion. Sauté 4 minutes.

Meanwhile, combine eggs, pepper and steak sauce in bowl. Stir in ham mixture; mix until blended.

Pour about ⅓ c. of the egg mixture into skillet over medium heat, forming 4″ pattie. Cook 1½ minutes. Turn over and cook 1½ minutes more or until golden brown. Remove from skillet and keep warm. Repeat with remaining egg mixture, making 3 more omelets, about 9 minutes.

Serve each omelet between 2 slices of buttered toast.

Makes 4 servings.

47/Cheesy egg puff

- *Preparation time: 2 minutes*
- *Cooking time: 28 minutes*

This recipe is a combination of a creamy quiche and an omelet all in one—perfect for supper or brunch. (See photo, Plate 7.)

4 eggs	½ c. tomato paste or
2 c. milk	tomato sauce
¾ c. flour	¼ tsp. dried oregano
¾ tsp. salt	leaves
½ tsp. paprika	¼ tsp. dried basil leaves
¼ tsp. pepper	2 tblsp. cooking oil
6 strips bacon	1 c. shredded Cheddar
1 c. finely chopped	cheese
onion	Minced fresh parsley

Measure first 6 ingredients.

Fry bacon in 10″ skillet over medium heat until browned, about 5 minutes. Remove bacon and drain on paper towels. Crumble bacon.

Meanwhile, lightly beat eggs in bowl with fork or whisk. Add milk and blend well. Stir in flour, salt, paprika and pepper. (Mixture will not be smooth.)

Cut and measure remaining ingredients.

Pour off all but 1 tblsp. bacon drippings. Sauté onion in bacon drippings over medium heat 3 minutes. Remove from heat. Stir in tomato paste, oregano and basil. Pour into a bowl and rinse out skillet.

Heat oil in same skillet over medium heat, about 1 minute. Pour egg batter into skillet. Reduce heat to medium low. Cover and cook 10 minutes.

Spread top of egg mixture with sauce mixture and sprinkle with bacon and cheese. Reduce heat to low. Cover and cook 9 minutes more.

Remove from heat. Let stand 5 minutes before serving. Cut into wedges and sprinkle with parsley.

Makes 6 servings.

48/Low-cal vegetable omelet

• *Preparation time: 6 minutes*
• *Cooking time: 24 minutes*

A Virginia farm woman wrote at the bottom of this recipe, "I serve this often because it's fairly low in calories and fun to make."

1 c. pared carrot strips, 2" lengths	$\frac{1}{8}$ tsp. salt
½ c. sliced onion	8 eggs
3 tblsp. butter or regular margarine	¼ c. milk
1 c. sliced fresh mushrooms	½ tsp. salt
	⅛ tsp. pepper
	2 tblsp. butter or regular margarine

Cut and measure carrots and onion.

Melt 3 tblsp. butter in 10" skillet over medium heat, about 3 minutes.

Meanwhile, slice mushrooms.

Add carrots, onion, mushrooms and ⅛ tsp. salt to skillet. Sauté 10 minutes or until tender.

Meanwhile, measure remaining ingredients. Combine eggs, milk, ½ tsp. salt and pepper in bowl. Beat with rotary beater until blended.

Remove vegetables to another bowl from skillet. Melt 2 tblsp. butter in same skillet over low heat, about 1 minute.

Pour eggs into skillet. As egg mixture sets, lift with spatula to allow uncooked portions to flow to bottom of skillet. Cook 10 minutes or until egg is completely set. Loosen edges of omelet. Spoon cooked vegetables over omelet. Fold in half and remove to serving platter.

Makes 4 servings.

49/Creamed eggs and chipped beef

- *Preparation time: 10 minutes*
- *Cooking time: 20 minutes*

Two brunch favorites, goldenrod eggs and creamed chipped beef, are combined in one. Delicious on rice as well as toast.

6 hard-cooked eggs
6 tblsp. butter or regular margarine
1 (4-oz.) pkg. dried or smoked beef, cut up
6 tblsp. flour
¼ tsp. dry mustard
¼ tsp. Worcestershire sauce
⅛ tsp. pepper
3¼ c. milk
9 slices bread, toasted and cut in half diagonally

Cut and measure all ingredients before starting to cook.

Remove yolks from eggs and press through sieve. Chop egg whites.

Melt butter in 10″ skillet over medium heat, about 1 minute.

Add dried beef to skillet. Cook, stirring constantly, 5 minutes. Stir in flour, dry mustard, Worcestershire sauce and pepper.

Gradually stir in milk. Cook, stirring constantly, until mixture boils and thickens, about 10 minutes.

Stir in chopped egg whites and heat 4 minutes.

Serve over toast and garnish with sieved yolks.

Makes 6 servings.

50/Welsh rabbit

• *Preparation time: 9 minutes*
• *Cooking time: 12 minutes*

The cheese won't curdle in this Welsh rabbit recipe because it's gradually stirred into a white sauce base.

⅓ c. butter or regular
  margarine
⅓ c. flour
¼ tsp. salt
¼ tsp. dry mustard
⅛ tsp. pepper
2¼ c. milk
1 tsp. Worcestershire
  sauce

2 drops Tabasco sauce
2½ c. shredded sharp
  Cheddar cheese (10 oz.)
12 slices bread, toasted
2 medium tomatoes,
  sliced
Chopped fresh parsley

Melt butter in 10″ skillet over medium heat, about 2 minutes. Stir in flour, salt, dry mustard and pepper. Gradually stir in milk. Then add Worcestershire sauce and Tabasco sauce. Cook 5 minutes, stirring constantly, until mixture comes to a boil.

Gradually stir in cheese. Cook, stirring constantly, until cheese is melted, about 5 minutes. Serve over toast. Garnish with tomato slices and chopped parsley.

Makes 6 servings.

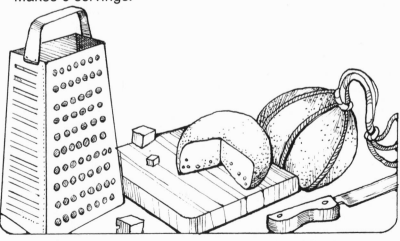

51/Broccoli and zucchini with noodles

- *Preparation time: 7 minutes*
- *Cooking time: 23 minutes*

This delightfully different vegetable main dish combines broccoli with zucchini in cheese sauce served over spinach noodles.

¾ c. water
½ tsp. salt
1 (10-oz.) pkg. frozen broccoli spears, thawed and cut into 1″ pieces
2 c. cubed unpared zucchini (½″)
2 tblsp. butter or regular margarine
½ c. chopped onion
1 clove garlic, minced
3 tblsp. flour

1 c. milk
2 tblsp. chopped fresh parsley
½ tsp. salt
½ tsp. dried oregano leaves
1½ c. creamed small-curd cottage cheese
1 c. shredded Swiss cheese
8 oz. spinach noodles, cooked and drained

Cut and measure all ingredients before starting to cook.

Heat water and ½ tsp. salt in 10″ skillet over high heat until it comes to a boil, about 1 minute. Add broccoli and zucchini. Return to a boil, about 1 minute. Reduce heat to medium. Cover and cook 9 minutes. Drain well in colander.

Melt butter in same skillet over medium-high heat, about 1 minute. Add onion and garlic; sauté 4 minutes.

Stir in flour. Gradually stir in milk. Add parsley, ½ tsp. salt and oregano. Cook, stirring constantly, until mixture boils and thickens, about 1 minute.

Reduce heat to medium. Stir in cottage cheese. Cook, stirring constantly, until almost melted, about 2 minutes. Add Swiss cheese. Cook and stir until melted, about 2 minutes.

Add broccoli and zucchini. Cook 2 minutes or until thoroughly heated. Ladle broccoli mixture over noodles.

Makes 6 servings.

52/Summer squash and zucchini

• *Preparation time: 12 minutes*
• *Cooking time: 18 minutes*

This versatile recipe can be served as a main dish or side dish. Just before serving, sprinkle with freshly grated Parmesan cheese.

8 strips bacon, diced
2 c. green pepper strips
1 c. sliced onion
1 lb. zucchini, sliced
1 lb. yellow summer
    squash, sliced
1 chicken bouillon cube

1 tsp. dried basil leaves
½ tsp. salt
⅛ tsp. pepper
½ c. water
2 large tomatoes, cut in
    wedges
Grated Parmesan cheese

Fry bacon in 12″ skillet or electric frypan over medium heat (350⁰) 5 minutes or until browned. Remove bacon from skillet with slotted spoon and drain on paper towels.

Pour off all but 3 tblsp. of the bacon drippings. Add green pepper strips, onion, zucchini and summer squash. Cook over medium heat (350⁰) 5 minutes, stirring constantly.

Stir in chicken bouillon cube, basil, salt, pepper and water. Bring mixture to a boil, about 1 minute.

Reduce heat to low (220⁰). Cover and simmer 5 minutes or until squash is tender.

Add tomato wedges and bacon. Heat 2 minutes more. Serve with grated Parmesan cheese.

Makes 4 to 6 servings.

2 Easy stir-fried dishes

A book of skillet cookery wouldn't be complete without a sampling of stir-fried dishes. This classic Chinese technique has become increasingly popular as more people begin to appreciate the convenience, the tender-crisp texture and the natural bright colors of stir-fried foods.

"My family just loves this chicken chop suey—it adds variety to the menu and a touch of elegance. It looks as if I spent all day in the kitchen, but it actually takes 25 minutes at the most," wrote an Iowa farm wife whose recipe is included in this chapter.

If you haven't already tried stir-frying, it's a simple technique to learn. First, all the ingredients must be cut into uniformly shaped pieces. In each recipe, we tell you exactly how to do this. Vegetables often are cut on the bias, exposing as much surface area as possible, so that they will cook quickly and evenly.

The second step is to sear the ingredients quickly in hot oil, starting with the ones that require the longest cooking period. In some recipes, meat or fish is removed and returned to the skillet later in order to prevent overcooking.

You don't need special equipment to cook these dishes; an ordinary skillet or electric frypan will do. However, most of the recipes can be adapted to an electric wok if you're lucky enough to own one. Just use the temperatures indicated for the electric frypan. The traditional nonelectric wok works fine, too.

We found that a wooden spoon works well for stirring, but if you're more adventuresome, try using a long pair of chopsticks.

54/Chinese beef with vegetables

- *Preparation time: 23 minutes*
- *Cooking time: 24 minutes*

If you've never tried to stir-fry before, start with this basic recipe. It's brightly colored and appeals to most palates.

1 lb. beef flank steak
3 tblsp. cooking oil
½ lb. fresh mushrooms, sliced
1 medium onion, sliced
½ c. bias-cut celery, ¼″ slices
1 clove garlic, minced
½ c. water

3 tblsp. soy sauce
½ tsp. beef bouillon granules
1 (6-oz.) pkg. frozen pea pods, thawed
1 pt. cherry tomatoes
1 tblsp. cornstarch
2 tblsp. water
Hot cooked rice

Cut and measure all ingredients before starting to cook.

Cut flank steak lengthwise into strips 2″ wide. Then slice meat across the grain into thin slices.

Heat oil in 12″ skillet or electric frypan over medium-high heat (375⁰) 5 minutes or until hot.

Add beef and stir-fry 7 minutes. Push beef to one side of skillet. Add mushrooms, onion, celery, garlic, ½ c. water, soy sauce and bouillon granules.

Cook until mixture comes to a boil, about 2 minutes.

Reduce heat to low (220⁰). Cover and simmer 5 minutes.

Add pea pods and tomatoes. Cover and simmer 3 minutes.

Combine cornstarch and 2 tblsp. water in small bowl; stir to blend. Stir cornstarch mixture into skillet. Cook, stirring constantly, until mixture boils and thickens, about 2 minutes. Serve with rice.

Makes 6 servings.

55/Beef with onions and zucchini

- *Preparation time: 20 minutes*
- *Cooking time: 20 minutes*

Whether or not you add the bean curd, you won't be disappointed with this attractive dish featuring strips of zucchini and sirloin.

1 lb. boneless beef sirloin
  steak
$\frac{1}{8}$ tsp. pepper
4 tblsp. cooking oil
1 clove garlic, minced
6 medium onions, cut into
  wedges
2 tsp. beef bouillon
  granules
1 c. water

2 c. unpared zucchini
  strips, $2 \times \frac{1}{4}$" pieces
$\frac{1}{4}$ tsp. browning for gravy
1 (19-oz.) can bean curd,
  drained and cut into $\frac{1}{2}$"
  cubes
2 tblsp. cornstarch
3 tblsp. soy sauce
Hot cooked rice

Cut and measure all ingredients before starting to cook.

Cut beef into $2 \times \frac{1}{8}$" strips. Season with pepper.

Heat 2 tblsp. of the oil in 12" skillet or electric frypan over medium heat (325^0) 5 minutes.

Add beef and garlic. Stir-fry 4 minutes. Remove from skillet. Heat remaining 2 tblsp. oil in skillet 1 minute.

Add onion and stir-fry 2 minutes. Add beef bouillon granules and water. Cook until mixture comes to a boil, about 1 minute. Reduce heat to low (220^0). Cover and simmer 3 minutes, stirring occasionally.

Add zucchini. Cover and simmer 2 minutes, stirring occasionally.

Stir in meat, browning for gravy and bean curd. Combine cornstarch and soy sauce; stir to blend. Stir cornstarch mixture into skillet. Cook, stirring constantly, until mixture boils and thickens, about 2 minutes. Serve with rice.

Makes 4 servings.

56/Classic sukiyaki

* Preparation time: 30 minutes
* Cooking time: 17 minutes

If you want to impress your guests, serve this classic version of sukiyaki. Cook it at the table and serve each guest individually.

1 lb. boneless beef sirloin steak
½ lb. fresh mushrooms, sliced
1½ c. bias-cut pared carrots, ⅛" slices
1 c. bias-cut celery, ¼" slices
12 green onions and tops, cut into 2" pieces

1 (10-oz.) pkg. fresh spinach, washed and trimmed (4 c.)
½ c. beef broth
⅓ c. soy sauce
¼ c. dry sherry
2 tblsp. sugar
2 tblsp. cooking oil
Hot cooked rice

Cut and measure all ingredients before starting to cook.

Cut beef into 2 × ¼" strips. Arrange meat strips, mushrooms, carrots, celery, green onions and spinach in a decorative pattern on a large plate or platter.

Combine beef broth, soy sauce, sherry and sugar in a small pitcher. Heat 1 tblsp. of the oil in 12" electric frypan over medium heat (325º) 5 minutes or until hot.

Add one half of the meat to hot oil. Stir-fry 2 minutes. Push meat to one corner of skillet. Then add one half of the mushrooms, one half of the carrots, one half of the celery and one half of the green onions, keeping each vegetable separate from the others. Pour one half of soy sauce mixture over vegetables. Stir-fry 3 minutes, keeping vegetables separate. Add one half of the spinach and stir-fry until wilted, about 1 minute.

Serve guests a sampling of meat and vegetables with rice. Heat remaining 1 tblsp. oil in skillet. Add remaining meat and vegetables and stir-fry as before, about 6 minutes.

Makes 4 servings.

Plate 1: Fresh broccoli and mushrooms are the main ingredients in Oriental Stir-Fried Vegetables (p. 90). Chinese vegetables and pea pods round out the dish.

Plate 2: Country-style Pork Chop Skillet Dinner (p. 125) features tender chops with potatoes and carrot chunks in a flavorful gravy for a nourishing one-dish meal.

Plate 3: This timesaving
main dish is special enough
for company. Curried Chicken
Skillet (p. 22) can be
prepared and simmered to
perfection in just 30 minutes.

Plate 4: A family-style meal that's a snap to prepare, Quick Ham-Macaroni Skillet (p. 20) is an extra-creamy, nutritious macaroni dish with lots of Cheddar cheese.

57/American-style steak with green beans

- *Preparation time: 19 minutes*
- *Cooking time: 28 minutes*

One of our test kitchen home economists developed this stir-fried recipe using steak, green beans and tomatoes seasoned with basil.

1 lb. boneless beef sirloin
  steak
½ tsp. salt
⅛ tsp. pepper
3 tblsp. cooking oil
½ lb. fresh green beans,
  cut into 1″ diagonal
  slices
1 c. chopped onion
2 cloves garlic, minced

½ c. water
2 beef bouillon cubes,
  crumbled
1 tsp. dried basil leaves
½ tsp. salt
1 tblsp. cornstarch
2 tblsp. water
2 medium tomatoes,
  peeled and diced
½ tsp. browning for gravy

Cut and measure all ingredients before starting to cook. Thinly slice beef into 2½ × ¼″ strips. Season with ½ tsp. salt and pepper.

Heat 2 tblsp. of the oil in 12″ skillet or electric frypan over medium heat (350⁰) 5 minutes.

Add beef. Stir-fry 3 minutes or until meat changes color. Remove beef from skillet. Add remaining 1 tblsp. oil to skillet. Heat 2 minutes or until hot.

Add green beans, onion and garlic. Stir-fry 1 minute. Add ½ c. water, beef bouillon cubes, basil and ½ tsp. salt. Reduce heat to low (220⁰). Cover and simmer 15 minutes or until beans are tender.

Combine cornstarch and 2 tblsp. water in small bowl; stir until blended.

Add cornstarch mixture, beef and tomatoes to skillet. Stir in browning for gravy. Cook, stirring constantly, until mixture boils and thickens, about 2 minutes.

Makes 6 servings.

58/Beef with pea pods

• *Preparation time: 18 minutes*
• *Cooking time: 12 minutes*

This beef recipe features fresh mushrooms, pea pods, crunchy water chestnuts and green onions flavored with a little sherry.

1 lb. boneless beef
   sirloin steak
3 tblsp. cooking oil
1 tblsp. sesame oil
1 clove garlic, minced
½ lb. fresh mushrooms,
   sliced
2 (6-oz.) pkg. frozen pea
   pods, thawed
1 (8-oz.) can water
   chestnuts, drained and
   sliced

½ c. sliced green onions
2 tblsp. cornstarch
½ c. beef broth
¼ c. dry sherry
2 tblsp. soy sauce
¼ tsp. ground ginger
Hot cooked rice

Cut and measure all ingredients before starting to cook. Cut beef into $2 \times \frac{1}{4}''$ strips.

Heat oil and sesame oil in 12″ skillet or electric frypan over medium heat (325⁰) 5 minutes.

Add one half of the beef and garlic to hot oil. Stir-fry 1 minute. Push beef to sides of skillet. Add remaining beef and stir-fry 1 minute. Mix beef together. Continue stir-frying 2 minutes.

Add mushrooms, pea pods, water chestnuts and green onions. Stir-fry 1 minute.

Combine cornstarch, beef broth, sherry, soy sauce and ginger in small bowl; stir to blend. Stir cornstarch mixture into skillet. Cook until mixture comes to a boil, stirring constantly, about 1 minute. Boil 1 minute. Serve with rice.

Makes 6 servings.

59/Oriental pepper steak

This is one of the more popular dishes in Chinese restaurants in America because it's seasoned to the average person's taste.

1½ lb. boneless beef sirloin steak	1 tblsp. sesame oil
½ c. beef broth	1 clove garlic, minced
2 tblsp. cornstarch	1 medium onion, sliced
1 tsp. paprika	2 medium green peppers, cut into ¼" strips
¼ tsp. ground ginger	16 cherry tomatoes, halved
¼ c. soy sauce	Hot cooked rice
3 tblsp. cooking oil	

Cut and measure all ingredients before starting to cook.

Cut beef into 3 × ⅛" strips. Combine beef broth, cornstarch, paprika, ginger and soy sauce in small bowl; stir to blend. Set aside.

Heat oil and sesame oil in 12" skillet or electric frypan over medium heat (325⁰) 5 minutes.

Add beef, one-third at a time, stir-fry 1 minute. Push to side of skillet. Repeat with remaining beef, about 2 minutes.

Add garlic and onion and stir-fry 2 minutes. Add green pepper. Cover and cook 2 minutes.

Add tomatoes and stir-fry 2 minutes. Stir in cornstarch mixture. Cook until mixture comes to a boil, stirring constantly, about 1 minute. Boil 1 minute more.

Serve with rice.

Makes 6 servings.

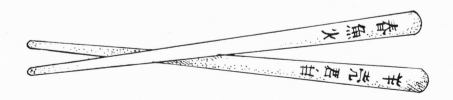

60/Chinese beef with water chestnuts

- *Preparation time: 23 minutes*
- *Cooking time: 19 minutes*

"My family likes this for its crispness and tastiness. It can be prepared quickly and is low in calories," wrote a farm woman.

1 lb. boneless beef sirloin steak
2 (3-oz.) cans sliced mushrooms
⅓ c. soy sauce
½ c. beef broth
4 tblsp. cooking oil
2 c. bias-cut celery, ⅛" slices
2 c. bias-cut green onions, 1" pieces

1 c. green pepper strips
1 (8-oz.) can water chestnuts, drained and sliced
1 tblsp. sugar
½ tsp. browning for gravy
8 tsp. cornstarch
¼ c. water
Hot cooked rice

Cut and measure all ingredients before starting to cook.

Cut steak into 2½ × ⅛" strips. Drain mushrooms, reserving liquid. Combine reserved mushroom liquid with soy sauce and beef broth. Set aside.

Heat 2 tblsp. of the cooking oil in 12" skillet or electric frypan over medium heat (325⁰) 5 minutes.

Add beef and stir-fry 3 minutes. Remove from skillet.

Heat remaining 2 tblsp. oil in skillet 1 minute. Add celery and stir-fry 1 minute. Stir in soy sauce mixture. Cook until mixture comes to a boil, stirring constantly, about 2 minutes. Cover and simmer 2 minutes more. Add green onions, green pepper and water chestnuts. Cover and cook 2 minutes.

Add beef, mushrooms, sugar and browning for gravy. Combine cornstarch and water in small bowl; stir to blend. Stir cornstarch mixture into skillet. Cook until mixture comes to a boil, stirring constantly, about 1 minute. Boil 2 minutes more. Serve with rice.

Makes 6 servings.

61/Hamburger stir-fry

- *Preparation time: 10 minutes*
- *Cooking time: 18 minutes*

A Wisconsin homemaker told us, "My son first raved about this 20 years ago at a 4-H supper. I've made it ever since."

1 lb. ground chuck
1 c. chopped onion
1 c. green pepper strips
5 medium carrots, cut into
   1½" strips
½ c. chopped celery
1 clove garlic, minced
½ tsp. salt
⅛ tsp. pepper

1 (16-oz.) can bean
   sprouts, drained
1 (10-oz.) pkg. frozen peas,
   thawed
1 c. water
2 tblsp. cornstarch
4 tblsp. soy sauce
2 tblsp. water
½ tsp. browning for gravy

Cut and measure all ingredients before starting to cook.

Heat 12" skillet or electric frypan over medium heat (350º) 5 minutes or until hot.

Add ground chuck, onion, green pepper, carrots, celery, garlic, salt and pepper. Stir-fry 5 minutes or until meat is well browned.

Add bean sprouts, peas and 1 c. water. Cook until mixture comes to a boil, about 1 minute. Reduce heat to low (220º). Cover and simmer 5 minutes.

Combine cornstarch, soy sauce, 2 tblsp. water and browning for gravy in small bowl; stir to blend.

Stir cornstarch mixture into skillet. Cook over medium heat (350º), stirring constantly, until mixture boils and thickens, about 2 minutes.

Makes 6 servings.

62/Ground beef sukiyaki

- *Preparation time: 5 minutes*
- *Cooking time: 19 minutes*

"Since we now grow our own snow peas, I added them to the original recipe that I got from my sister," said an Illinois woman.

1 lb. ground chuck
1 c. bias-cut celery, $\frac{1}{8}$"
   slices
$\frac{1}{2}$ c. chopped onion
1 (16-oz.) can bean
   sprouts, drained
1 (8-oz.) can sliced water
   chestnuts, drained
1 (4-oz.) can sliced
   mushrooms

2 beef bouillon cubes
1 c. boiling water
$\frac{1}{2}$ tsp. salt
3 tblsp. soy sauce
3 tblsp. cornstarch
$\frac{1}{4}$ c. water
$\frac{1}{2}$ tsp. browning for gravy
1 (6-oz.) pkg. frozen pea
   pods, thawed
Hot cooked rice

Cut and measure all ingredients before starting to cook.

Cook ground chuck, celery and onion in 12" skillet or electric frypan over medium heat (350⁰) 5 minutes or until meat is browned and onion is tender.

Stir in bean sprouts, water chestnuts, undrained mushrooms, beef bouillon cubes and 1 c. boiling water. Reduce heat to low (220⁰). Cover and simmer 10 minutes.

Combine salt, soy sauce, cornstarch, $\frac{1}{4}$ c. water and browning for gravy in small bowl. Stir to blend. Add cornstarch mixture to skillet. Cook until mixture comes to a boil, stirring constantly, until mixture boils and thickens, about 2 minutes.

Stir in pea pods. Cook 2 minutes more. Serve with rice.

Makes 6 servings.

63/Ground beef chop suey

• *Preparation time: 8 minutes*
• *Cooking time: 48 minutes*

Although dishes containing ground beef aren't really Chinese in origin, this meat adapts well to this fast method of cooking.

3 tblsp. cooking oil
1½ c. sliced celery
1 c. green pepper strips
1 large onion, cut into 8 wedges
1 clove garlic, minced
1 lb. ground chuck
1 tsp. salt

⅛ tsp. pepper
2 tblsp. soy sauce
1¼ c. water
2 tblsp. cornstarch
¼ c. water
2 c. boiling water
1 c. uncooked regular rice
½ tsp. salt

Cut and measure all ingredients before starting to cook.

Heat oil in 12″ skillet or electric frypan over medium heat (350⁰) 5 minutes.

Add celery, green pepper, onion and garlic to hot oil. Stir-fry 8 minutes or until tender-crisp. Remove from skillet.

Add ground chuck and fry until well browned, about 10 minutes. Stir in 1 tsp. salt, pepper, soy sauce, 1¼ c. water and onion mixture. Combine cornstarch and ¼ c. water in small bowl; stir to blend. Stir cornstarch mixture into meat mixture. Cook, stirring constantly, until mixture boils and thickens, about 5 minutes.

Push meat mixture to sides of skillet. Pour 2 c. boiling water into center. Stir in rice and ½ tsp. salt. Reduce heat to low (220⁰). Cover and simmer 20 minutes or until rice is tender.

Makes 4 to 6 servings.

Note: This recipe cannot be made in a wok.

64/Hamburger broccoli skillet

• Preparation time: 8 minutes
• Cooking time: 43 minutes

This isn't really a typical stir-fry recipe because it takes so long to cook the regular and wild rice mix used in it.

1 lb. fresh broccoli
1 lb. ground chuck
¼ c. chopped onion
¼ c. chopped green pepper
1 beef bouillon cube, crumbled

1 (6-oz.) pkg. long-grain and wild rice mix
2½ c. water
1 tblsp. soy sauce

Cut and measure all ingredients before starting to cook.

Remove flowerets from broccoli and cut in half. Cut stems into 1″ pieces.

Brown ground chuck in 10″ skillet over medium-high heat 5 minutes. Remove from skillet with slotted spoon.

Add onion and green pepper to pan drippings. Stir-fry 5 minutes.

Add bouillon cube, rice mix and water. Cook until mixture comes to a boil, stirring constantly, about 3 minutes. Reduce heat to low. Cover and simmer 10 minutes.

Stir in cooked meat and broccoli. Cover and simmer 20 minutes or until rice and broccoli are tender.

Add soy sauce and stir well.

Makes 6 servings.

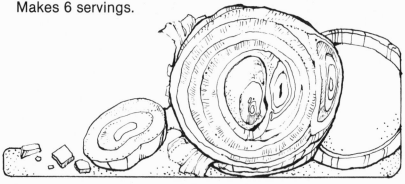

65/Curried pork with rice

• *Preparation time: 21 minutes*
• *Cooking time: 24 minutes*

This is an American recipe using the stir-fry method. Good served with condiments such as raisins, coconut and chopped onion.

1 lb. boneless pork steak
5 tblsp. butter or regular
   margarine
2 c. chopped onion
1 large apple, cored and
   thinly sliced
1½ c. apple juice

1 tblsp. cornstarch
1½ tsp. curry powder
1 tsp. salt
2 tblsp. sweet pickle relish
Hot cooked rice
½ c. coarsely chopped
   peanuts

Cut and measure all ingredients before starting to cook.

Cut pork into 2 × ⅛" strips.

Heat 12" skillet or electric frypan over medium heat (350°) 5 minutes or until hot.

Melt 4 tblsp. of the butter in skillet, about 1 minute.

Add pork and stir-fry 5 minutes. Remove pork from skillet. Reduce heat to medium-low (300°). Melt remaining 1 tblsp. butter in skillet, about 1 minute.

Add onion and stir-fry 3 minutes. Add apple and stir-fry 2 minutes.

Combine apple juice, cornstarch, curry powder and salt in small bowl. Stir to blend. Stir cornstarch mixture into skillet. Cook, stirring constantly, until mixture boils and thickens, about 2 minutes. Stir in pork and pickle relish. Reduce heat to low (220°).

Cover and simmer 5 minutes. Serve over hot rice and sprinkle with peanuts.

Makes 4 servings.

66/**Pork fried rice**

• *Preparation time: 23 minutes*
• *Cooking time: 18 minutes*

To save last-minute preparation time, cut up the ingredients the night before and refrigerate until time to cook the meal.

1 lb. boneless lean pork	3 c. cooked regular rice
2 tblsp. cooking oil	3 tblsp. soy sauce
2 eggs	2 c. chopped fresh spinach
1 c. bias-cut celery, ⅛″ slices	½ c. chicken broth
1 c. coarsely diced green pepper	1 (6-oz.) pkg. frozen pea pods, thawed
½ c. chopped onion	⅛ tsp. salt
	⅛ tsp. pepper

Cut and measure all ingredients before starting to cook.

Cut pork into 2 × ¼″ strips.

Heat oil in 12″ skillet or electric frypan over medium heat (350⁰) 5 minutes.

Beat eggs in bowl with rotary beater until blended. Add to hot oil. Cook 1 minute, stirring frequently, until eggs are set. Remove eggs from skillet and set aside.

Add pork and celery. Stir-fry 5 minutes. Add green pepper and onion. Stir-fry 5 minutes or until vegetables are tender-crisp.

Stir in rice, soy sauce, spinach, chicken broth, pea pods, salt and pepper. Cook 2 minutes more or until hot.

Cut up cooked egg. Stir into rice mixture.

Makes 6 servings.

67/Oriental-style pork and vegetables

• *Preparation time: 22 minutes*
• *Cooking time: 20 minutes*

No rice is needed for this complete vegetable dish featuring pork strips, carrots, cabbage, water chestnuts and pea pods.

1 lb. boneless lean pork
4 tblsp. cooking oil
1 clove garlic, minced
$\frac{1}{8}$ tsp. pepper
2 c. bias-cut carrots, $\frac{1}{8}$"
  slices
2 medium onions, cut into
  wedges
3 c. shredded cabbage

1 (8-oz.) can water
  chestnuts, sliced and
  drained
1 c. chicken broth
2 tblsp. cornstarch
$\frac{1}{4}$ c. soy sauce
2 tblsp. dry sherry
1 (6-oz.) pkg. frozen pea
  pods, thawed

Cut and measure all ingredients before starting to cook.

Cut pork into $2 \times \frac{1}{8}$" strips.

Heat 2 tblsp. of the oil in 12" skillet or electric frypan over medium heat (325°) 5 minutes.

Add pork, garlic and pepper to hot oil. Stir-fry 5 minutes and remove from skillet.

Heat remaining 2 tblsp. oil in skillet 1 minute. Add carrots and stir-fry 2 minutes. Add onions and stir-fry 1 minute.

Add cabbage, water chestnuts and chicken broth. Cook until mixture comes to a boil, about 1 minute. Reduce heat to low (220°). Cover and simmer 3 minutes.

Combine cornstarch, soy sauce and sherry in small bowl; stir to blend.

Stir cornstarch mixture, pork and pea pods into skillet. Cook until mixture comes to a boil, stirring constantly, 1 minute. Boil 1 minute.

Makes 4 servings.

EASY STIR-FRIED DISHES

68/Pork with noodles

- *Preparation time: 24 minutes*
- *Cooking time: 13 minutes*

If your family doesn't like rice, here's the Chinese pork dish for your recipe file. It's served over hot cooked noodles.

1 lb. boneless lean pork
2 tblsp. cooking oil
1 clove garlic, minced
1 (10-oz.) pkg. frozen
  French-style green
  beans, thawed
2 c. bias-cut celery, ¼"
  slices
1 c. thinly sliced green
  onions

3 tblsp. cornstarch
¼ tsp. ground ginger
⅛ tsp. pepper
3 tblsp. soy sauce
1½ c. chicken broth
8 oz. medium noodles,
  cooked and drained

Cut and measure all ingredients before starting to cook.
Cut pork into 2 × ⅛" strips.

Heat oil in 12" skillet or electric frypan over medium heat (350⁰) 5 minutes.

Add one half of the pork and garlic; stir-fry 1 minute. Push to one side of skillet. Add remaining pork; stir-fry 1 minute. Mix all pork together. Continue stir-frying 3 minutes more.

Add green beans, celery and green onions. Stir-fry 1 minute.

Combine cornstarch, ginger, pepper, soy sauce and chicken broth in small bowl; stir to blend.

Stir in cornstarch mixture. Cook until mixture comes to a boil, stirring constantly, about 1 minute. Cook, stirring constantly, 1 minute more.

Serve over cooked noodles.

Makes 6 servings.

69/Chinese pork with vegetables

• Preparation time: 28 minutes
• Cooking time: 17 minutes

A pound of pork stretches to make six generous servings—an economical main dish. Serve with fried rice for a change.

1 lb. boneless pork steak
3 tblsp. soy sauce
¼ tsp. ground ginger
1 (4-oz.) can mushroom
  stems and pieces
Water
2 tblsp. cornstarch
1 tsp. chicken bouillon
  granules
5 tblsp. cooking oil

1½ c. bias-cut carrots,
  ⅛" slices
3 tblsp. water
1 (6-oz.) pkg. frozen pea
  pods, thawed
1½ c. thinly sliced
  cauliflower
6 green onions and tops,
  cut into ½" pieces
Hot cooked rice

Cut and measure all ingredients before starting to cook.

Cut pork into 2 × ⅛" strips. Combine pork strips, soy sauce and ginger in bowl; let stand while preparing other ingredients. Drain mushrooms, reserving liquid. Add enough water to liquid to make ½ c. Combine ½ c. liquid with cornstarch and bouillon granules in small bowl; set aside.

Heat 3 tblsp. of the oil in 12" skillet or electric frypan over medium-high heat (375⁰) 5 minutes or until hot.

Add pork mixture and stir-fry until all pink is gone, about 2 minutes. Push to one side of skillet. Add carrots and stir-fry 2 minutes. Stir pork and carrots together. Add 3 tblsp. water. Cover and cook 2 minutes. Remove mixture from skillet.

Add remaining 2 tblsp. oil to skillet and heat 1 minute.

Stir in mushrooms, pea pods, cauliflower and green onions. Stir-fry 3 minutes. Return meat mixture to skillet. Stir in cornstarch mixture. Cook, stirring constantly, until mixture boils and thickens, about 2 minutes. Serve with rice.

Makes 6 servings.

70/Sweet-and-sour pork

• *Preparation time: 20 minutes*
• *Cooking time: 18 minutes*

This sweet-and-sour dish is more American than Chinese. Mixed sweet pickles give it an interesting flavor, texture and color.

¾ lb. boneless lean pork
1 (20-oz.) can sliced
   pineapple in juice
Water
¼ c. brown sugar, packed
2 tblsp. cornstarch
½ tsp. salt
¼ c. vinegar

3 tblsp. cooking oil
1 green pepper, cut into
   long strips
12 green onions and tops,
   cut into 1″ pieces
⅓ c. mixed sweet pickles,
   sliced
Hot cooked rice

Cut and measure all ingredients before starting to cook.

Cut pork into 2 × ⅛″ strips. Drain pineapple, reserving juice. Add enough water to juice to make 1 c. Combine 1 c. juice with brown sugar, cornstarch, salt, and vinegar in small bowl. Stir to blend. Set aside. Cut pineapple slices in eighths and set aside.

Heat oil in 12″ skillet or electric frypan over medium-high heat (375⁰) 5 minutes or until hot.

Add pork and stir-fry 3 minutes. Add green pepper and stir-fry 1 minute. Add onions and stir-fry 2 minutes.

Stir in cornstarch mixture. Cook, stirring constantly, until mixture boils and thickens, about 2 minutes. Add pineapple and mixed pickles. Reduce heat to low (220⁰). Cover and simmer 5 minutes or until green pepper and onion are tender-crisp. Serve with rice.

Makes 4 servings.

71/Pork-broccoli stir-fry

- *Preparation time: 30 minutes*
- *Cooking time: 23 minutes*

This Oriental-style recipe was sent to us by a Missouri farm woman who makes it often for her family.

1 lb. boneless lean pork	1 c. water
1½ lb. fresh broccoli	2 tblsp. cooking oil
1 tblsp. cornstarch	1 clove garlic, minced
2 tsp. sugar	1½ c. sliced onion
⅛ tsp. ground ginger	1½ c. pared carrot strips,
⅛ tsp. pepper	2 × ¼" pieces
¼ c. soy sauce	Hot cooked rice

Cut and measure all ingredients before starting to cook.

Cut pork into 2 × ¼" strips. Remove flowerets from broccoli and cut in half. Cut stems into thin 2" strips.

Combine cornstarch, sugar, ginger, pepper, soy sauce and water in bowl; stir to blend. Set aside.

Heat oil in 12" skillet or electric frypan over medium heat (350°) 5 minutes.

Add pork, broccoli stalks and garlic to hot oil. Stir-fry 5 minutes. Add onion, carrots and broccoli flowerets. Stir-fry 5 minutes.

Stir cornstarch mixture into vegetable mixture. Cook, stirring constantly, until mixture comes to a boil, about 2 minutes. Boil 1 minute. Cover and cook 5 minutes or until vegetables are tender-crisp.

Serve with rice.

Makes 6 servings.

72/Cabbage with chopped ham

• *Preparation time: 15 minutes*
• *Cooking time: 13 minutes*

When you stir-fry cabbage rather than steam it for a long time, it has a fresher flavor, crunchier texture and brighter color.

1 medium head cabbage, 2½ lb.	2 tblsp. chopped fresh parsley
3 tblsp. cooking oil	1 clove garlic, minced
½ c. chopped fully cooked ham	2 tsp. chicken bouillon granules
¼ c. chopped green onions and tops	½ tsp. salt
	⅓ c. water

Cut and measure all ingredients before starting to cook.

Cut cabbage in quarters; cut core and thickened parts from each leaf and discard. Tear cabbage leaves into 1 to 2″ pieces.

Heat oil in 12″ skillet or electric frypan over medium-high heat (375⁰) 5 minutes.

Add cabbage and stir-fry 1 minute. Reduce heat to low (220⁰). Add ham, green onions, parsley, garlic, chicken bouillon granules, salt and water. Cover and cook 5 minutes.

Uncover. Stir-fry cabbage mixture 2 minutes or until cabbage is tender-crisp.

Makes 8 servings.

73/Sweet-and-sour ham with pineapple

- *Preparation time: 18 minutes*
- *Cooking time: 21 minutes*

A mildly flavored sweet-and-sour dish featuring pineapple chunks, sliced carrots, zucchini, ham strips and sliced green onions.

1 lb. fully cooked ham
  steak
2 (8-oz.) cans pineapple
  chunks in juice
Water
4 tblsp. cooking oil
2 c. bias-cut pared
  carrots, 1/8" slices

2 1/2 c. bias-cut zucchini,
  1/8" slices
1/2 c. sliced green onions
3 tblsp. cornstarch
1/4 c. sugar
1/4 c. vinegar
1 tblsp. soy sauce
Hot cooked rice

Cut and measure all ingredients before starting to cook.

Cut ham into 2 × 1/8" strips.

Drain pineapple, reserving juice. Add enough water to juice to make 1 1/4 c. Set aside.

Heat 2 tblsp. of the oil in 12" skillet or electric frypan over medium heat (325°) 5 minutes.

Add ham. Stir-fry 2 minutes. Remove ham from skillet.

Add remaining 2 tblsp. oil to skillet and heat 1 minute.

Add carrots and stir-fry 2 minutes. Add 1 1/4 c. liquid to skillet. Cook until mixture comes to a boil, about 1 minute. Reduce heat to low (220°). Cover and simmer 5 minutes.

Add zucchini. Cover and simmer 3 minutes.

Stir in ham, pineapple chunks and green onions. Combine cornstarch, sugar, vinegar and soy sauce in small bowl; stir to blend. Stir cornstarch mixture into skillet. Cook, stirring constantly, until mixture comes to a boil, about 1 minute. Boil 1 minute. Serve with rice.

Makes 6 servings.

74/Almond chicken with broccoli

• Preparation time: 20 minutes
• Cooking time: 15 minutes

A lightly sauced dish with broccoli and mushrooms. Almonds are fried in hot oil to make them extra-crunchy.

2 (1-lb.) whole chicken breasts
2 (10-oz.) pkg. frozen broccoli spears, thawed
2 tblsp. cornstarch
¾ c. chicken broth
¼ c. soy sauce
1 c. cooking oil

½ c. whole blanched almonds
1 tblsp. sesame oil
¼ lb. fresh mushrooms, sliced
1 c. bias-cut celery, ⅛" slices

Cut and measure all ingredients before starting to cook.

Remove skin and bones from chicken. Cut into 1" cubes. Remove flowerets from broccoli and cut in half. Cut stalks into thin 1" strips.

Combine cornstarch, chicken broth and soy sauce in small bowl; stir until blended. Set aside.

Heat oil in electric wok over medium heat (365⁰) 5 minutes or until hot. Fry almonds, one half at a time, until golden brown. (Total cooking time: 3 minutes.) Remove almonds with a slotted spoon and drain on paper towels.

Remove all but 3 tblsp. oil from wok. Reduce heat to medium (325⁰). Add sesame oil and heat 1 minute.

Add chicken to hot oil. Stir-fry 2 minutes or until chicken becomes opaque. Add broccoli and stir-fry 1 minute. Add mushrooms and celery. Stir-fry 1 minute more.

Make a well in center of vegetables. Add cornstarch mixture. Cook, stirring constantly, until mixture boils and thickens, about 2 minutes. Sprinkle with almonds before serving.

Makes 6 servings.

75/Sweet-and-sour chicken

• Preparation time: 20 minutes
• Cooking time: 25 minutes

Each succulent piece of chicken is coated with batter and fried until golden brown and crisp. They're served in a sweet-and-sour sauce.

2 (1-lb.) whole chicken
 breasts
½ tsp. salt
1 egg, beaten
¾ c. buttermilk baking mix
1 c. cooking oil
⅔ c. sugar
2 tblsp. cornstarch
1 tblsp. paprika

1 (20-oz.) can pineapple
 chunks in juice
¼ c. soy sauce
¼ c. cider vinegar
1 c. green pepper strips
½ c. sliced onion
2 medium tomatoes, cut up
Hot cooked rice

Cut and measure all ingredients before starting to cook.

Remove skin and bones from chicken. Cut into 1″ chunks. Season chicken with salt. Dip into egg and then coat with baking mix.

Heat oil in 7″ skillet over medium heat to 400⁰ (use fat thermometer), about 3 minutes. Fry chicken, a little at a time, until golden brown. (Total cooking time: 10 minutes.) Remove chicken as it browns and drain on paper towels. Place chicken in 250⁰ oven to keep warm.

Combine sugar, cornstarch and paprika in 10″ skillet. Drain pineapple, reserving juice. Add enough water to juice to make 2 c. Stir 2 c. liquid, soy sauce and vinegar into skillet.

Cook over medium heat, stirring constantly, until mixture boils, about 3 minutes. Boil 1 minute.

Add green pepper and onion. Cover and simmer 5 minutes or until vegetables are tender-crisp. Add pineapple and tomatoes. Heat thoroughly, about 3 minutes. Stir in chicken and serve with rice.

Makes 6 to 8 servings.

76/California stir-fried chicken

- *Preparation time: 20 minutes*
- *Cooking time: 16½ minutes*

As you might expect, the vegetables remain bright-colored and tender-crisp in this dish. To serve, ladle over hot fluffy rice.

2 (1-lb.) whole chicken breasts
¼ c. soy sauce
1 (9-oz.) pkg. frozen French-style green beans, thawed
4 tsp. cornstarch
½ c. water
2 tblsp. chicken bouillon granules

5 tblsp. cooking oil
½ c. roasted cashew nuts
1½ c. bias-cut pared carrots, ⅛" slices
1 c. bias-cut celery, ⅛" slices
½ c. chopped onion
1 clove garlic, minced

Cut and measure all ingredients before starting to cook.

Remove skin and bones from chicken. Cut into 2 × ⅛" strips. Combine chicken and soy sauce in bowl. Blot green beans with paper towels. Combine cornstarch, water and bouillon granules in small bowl; stir to blend. Set aside.

Heat 2 tblsp. of the oil in 12" skillet or electric frypan over medium-high heat (375⁰) 5 minutes. Add cashews to oil; toast 30 seconds. Remove and drain on paper towels.

Add 1 more tblsp. oil to skillet. Add chicken mixture. Stir-fry 2 minutes or until opaque. Remove chicken. Add remaining 2 tblsp. oil. Add carrots. Cover and cook 1 minute.

Stir in celery, onion and garlic. Cover and cook 1 minute. Uncover and stir-fry 3 minutes or until vegetables are tender-crisp. Stir in chicken and cornstarch mixture. Cook, stirring constantly, until mixture boils and thickens, about 2 minutes. Add green beans and half of cashews. Cook just until beans are thoroughly heated, about 2 minutes. Serve topped with remaining cashews.

Makes 4 servings.

77/Stir-fried almond chicken

• Preparation time: 15 minutes
• Cooking time: 17 minutes

A Kentucky homemaker worked on this recipe again and again until she got the results she wanted. It's now a family favorite.

2 (1-lb.) whole chicken
  breasts
1 c. chicken broth
2 tblsp. cornstarch
4 tblsp. cooking oil
1¼ c. sliced blanched
  almonds

½ c. sliced green onions
2 tblsp. dry sherry
4 tsp. soy sauce
¼ tsp. ground ginger
Hot cooked rice

Cut and measure all ingredients before starting to cook.

Remove skin and bones from chicken. Cut into 2 x ¼" strips. Combine ¼ c. of the chicken broth and cornstarch in small bowl; stir to blend. Set aside.

Heat 2 tblsp. of the oil in 12" skillet or electric frypan over medium heat (350⁰) 5 minutes.

Add almonds. Cook 5 minutes, stirring constantly, or until almonds are golden brown. Remove almonds from skillet with slotted spoon and drain on paper towels.

Add remaining 2 tblsp. oil to skillet and heat 2 minutes. Add chicken and green onions. Stir-fry 2 minutes or until chicken becomes opaque.

Stir in sherry, soy sauce and ginger. Cook, stirring constantly, 2 minutes. Add 1 c. of the almonds, remaining ¾ c. chicken broth and cornstarch mixture. Cook, stirring constantly, until mixture boils and thickens, about 1 minute. Serve with rice and garnish with remaining almonds.

Makes 6 servings.

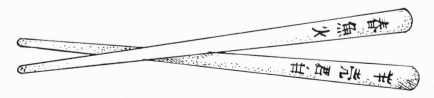

78/Chicken with garden vegetables

- *Preparation time: 25 minutes*
- *Cooking time: 17 minutes*

Stir-fried chicken dishes like this one are perfect for entertaining because they're easy to prepare, colorful and always so flavorful.

2 (1-lb.) whole chicken
   breasts
¼ tsp. salt
⅛ tsp. pepper
1 tblsp. cornstarch
1 tsp. brown sugar, packed
2 tblsp. soy sauce
1 tsp. cider vinegar
3 tblsp. cooking oil
3 small onions, cut
   into wedges

½ lb. fresh mushrooms,
   sliced
1 lb. zucchini, diagonally
   cut into ¼" slices
1 clove garlic, minced
2 chicken bouillon cubes
⅔ c. water
12 cherry tomatoes,
   halved

Cut and measure all ingredients before starting to cook.

Remove skin and bones from chicken. Cut into 1" cubes. Season with salt and pepper.

Combine cornstarch, brown sugar, soy sauce and vinegar in small bowl; stir to blend. Set aside.

Heat oil in 12" skillet or electric frypan over medium heat (325°) 5 minutes.

Add chicken to hot oil. Stir-fry 4 minutes or until chicken becomes opaque. Remove chicken from skillet.

Add onion and stir-fry 2 minutes. Add mushrooms, zucchini and garlic. Stir-fry 2 minutes. Add chicken bouillon cubes and water.

Reduce heat to low (220°). Cover and cook 2 minutes.

Stir in tomatoes, chicken and cornstarch mixture. Cook, stirring constantly, until mixture boils and thickens, about 2 minutes.

Makes 6 servings.

79/Chicken chow mein

• Preparation time: 23 minutes
• Cooking time: 15 minutes

Chow mein noodles add a pleasing crunchy note to this. If your family isn't fond of them, substitute plain white or fried rice.

2 (1-lb.) whole chicken
  breasts
¼ tsp. salt
2 tblsp. cooking oil
1 (5-oz.) can chow mein
  noodles
1½ c. bias-cut celery, ¼"
  slices
¼ lb. fresh mushrooms,
  sliced

2 c. shredded cabbage
1 c. chopped onion
1 (8-oz.) can sliced water
  chestnuts, drained
1½ c. chicken broth
3 tblsp. cornstarch
¼ c. soy sauce

Cut and measure all ingredients before starting to cook.

Remove skin and bones from chicken. Cut into 2 × ¼" strips. Season with salt.

Heat cooking oil in 12" skillet or electric frypan over medium heat (350°) 5 minutes. Meanwhile, place chow mein noodles in 9" square baking pan. Heat in 225° oven while preparing dish.

Add chicken to hot oil. Stir-fry 2 minutes or until chicken becomes opaque. Remove chicken from skillet. Add celery. Stir-fry 2 minutes.

Add mushrooms, cabbage, onion and water chestnuts. Stir-fry 2 minutes. Stir in chicken broth. Reduce heat to low (220°). Cover and simmer 3 minutes.

Combine cornstarch and soy sauce in small bowl; stir until blended.

Stir cornstarch mixture and chicken into skillet. Cook, stirring constantly, until thickened, about 1 minute. Serve over hot chow mein noodles.

Makes 6 servings.

80/Chinese-style chicken salad

• *Preparation time: 23 minutes*
• *Cooking time: 15 minutes*

A New York woman sent us this recipe "because it's delicious and is well liked by family and friends," she told us.

8 chicken thighs (2 lb.)
2 tblsp. cooking oil
1 tblsp. cornstarch
¼ c. soy sauce
¼ c. water
¼ tsp. salt
⅛ tsp. pepper
1 c. bias-cut celery,
** ¼″ slices**
1 clove garlic, minced

1 (8-oz.) can sliced water
** chestnuts, drained**
1 (4-oz.) can sliced
** mushrooms, drained**
½ c. sliced green onions
1 medium tomato, coarsely
** diced**
2 c. shredded iceberg
** lettuce**
Hot cooked rice

Cut and measure all ingredients before starting to cook.

Remove skin and bones from chicken. Cut into 1″ cubes.

Heat oil in 12″ skillet or electric frypan over medium heat (350⁰) 5 minutes.

Meanwhile, combine cornstarch, soy sauce, water, salt and pepper in small bowl; stir until blended. Set aside.

Add chicken, celery and garlic to hot oil. Stir-fry 3 minutes or until chicken becomes opaque.

Stir in water chestnuts, mushrooms and green onions. Stir-fry 3 minutes. Stir in cornstarch mixture. Cook until mixture comes to a boil, stirring constantly, about 1 minute. Boil 1 minute more.

Add tomato and lettuce. Cover and cook 2 minutes. Serve with rice.

Makes 6 servings.

81/Chicken chop suey

• *Preparation time: 25 minutes*
• *Cooking time: 24 minutes*

"My family just loves this. It adds variety to the menu and a touch of elegance. Fast, simple and delicious!" says an Iowa farm wife.

2 (1-lb.) whole chicken
  breasts
½ tsp. salt
4 tblsp. cooking oil
1 clove garlic, minced
3 c. bias-cut celery,
  ¼" slices
1½ c. chicken broth
3 medium onions, cut into
  wedges

1 (16-oz.) can bean
  sprouts, drained
1 (4-oz.) can sliced
  mushrooms, drained
¼ c. soy sauce
1 tsp. sugar
3 tblsp. cornstarch
1 tblsp. dry sherry
Hot cooked rice

Cut and measure all ingredients before starting to cook.

Remove skin and bones from chicken. Cut into 2 × ¼" strips. Season with salt.

Heat 2 tblsp. of the oil in 12" skillet or electric frypan over medium heat (325⁰) 5 minutes.

Add chicken and garlic. Stir-fry 3 minutes. Remove chicken from skillet.

Add remaining 2 tblsp. oil to skillet and heat 1 minute.

Add celery and stir-fry 1 minute. Add chicken broth. Bring to a boil, about 1 minute. Reduce heat to low (220⁰). Cover and cook 4 minutes.

Add onion. Cover and cook 6 minutes, stirring occasionally.

Stir in bean sprouts, mushrooms and chicken. Combine soy sauce, sugar, cornstarch and sherry in small bowl; stir to blend. Stir cornstarch mixture into skillet. Cook until mixture comes to a boil, stirring constantly, about 2 minutes. Boil 1 minute more. Serve with rice.

Makes 6 servings.

82/Chicken vegetable stir-fry

• *Preparation time: 22 minutes*
• *Cooking time: 20 minutes*

"This is my own version and is my husband's favorite—which says a lot from a meat-and-potatoes man," writes an Illinois farm woman.

2 (1-lb.) whole chicken
  breasts
¼ tsp. salt
3 tblsp. cooking oil
1 c. bias-cut celery,
  ¼" slices
1 c. sliced onion
1 c. chicken broth
2 tblsp. soy sauce

½ c. green pepper strips
1 (8-oz.) can water chestnuts, drained and sliced
1 (8-oz.) can bamboo
  shoots, drained
1 tblsp. cornstarch
2 tblsp. water
Hot cooked rice
Chow mein noodles

Cut and measure all ingredients before starting to cook.

Remove skin and bones from chicken. Cut into $2 \times \frac{1}{2}"$ strips. Season with salt.

Heat 2 tblsp. of the oil in 12" skillet or electric frypan over medium heat (325°) 5 minutes.

Add chicken. Stir-fry 3 minutes. Remove chicken from skillet.

Add remaining 1 tblsp. oil to skillet and heat 1 minute. Add celery and stir-fry 2 minutes. Add onion and stir-fry 1 minute.

Stir in chicken broth and soy sauce. Cook until mixture comes to a boil, about 1 minute. Reduce heat to low (220°). Cover and simmer 2 minutes.

Stir in green pepper, water chestnuts and bamboo shoots. Cover and simmer 3 minutes.

Combine cornstarch and water in small bowl; stir until blended. Stir cornstarch mixture and chicken into skillet. Cook, stirring constantly, until mixture boils and thickens, about 2 minutes. Serve over rice and top with chow mein noodles.

Makes 4 servings.

83/Ginger chicken

- *Preparation time: 25 minutes*
- *Cooking time: 20 minutes*

"The main advantage of this recipe is that it doesn't need other vegetables—it's complete in itself," a New Jersey woman told us.

2 (1-lb.) whole chicken breasts
¼ tsp. salt
⅛ tsp. pepper
½ medium bunch fresh broccoli
4 tblsp. cooking oil
2 medium onions, cut into wedges
½ c. bias-cut celery, ¼" slices
½ c. bias-cut pared carrots, ⅛" slices

¼ lb. fresh mushrooms, sliced
1 (8-oz.) can water chestnuts, drained and sliced
½ c. chicken broth
3 tblsp. dry sherry
3 tblsp. soy sauce
¼ tsp. ground ginger
1 tblsp. cornstarch
2 tblsp. water

Cut and measure all ingredients before starting to cook.

Remove skin and bones from chicken. Cut into $2 \times \frac{1}{4}$" strips. Season with salt and pepper. Remove flowerets from broccoli and cut stems into thin 2" strips.

Heat 2 tblsp. of the oil in 12" skillet or electric frypan over medium heat (325°) 5 minutes.

Add chicken and stir-fry 3 minutes or until chicken becomes opaque. Remove chicken from skillet.

Add remaining 2 tblsp. oil to skillet and heat 1 minute. Add onions, celery, carrots and broccoli. Stir-fry 2 minutes. Stir in mushrooms, water chestnuts, chicken broth, sherry, soy sauce and ginger. Cook until mixture comes to a boil, about 1 minute. Reduce heat to low (220°). Cover and simmer 5 minutes.

Combine cornstarch and water in bowl; stir until blended. Stir into skillet with chicken. Cook until it comes to a boil, stirring constantly, about 1 minute. Boil 2 minutes.

Makes 4 servings.

84/Chicken with green beans

- *Preparation time: 25 minutes*
- *Cooking time: 26 minutes*

You've never tasted green beans that are quite as good as stir-fried ones...the method preserves their natural color and fresh flavor.

2 (1-lb.) whole chicken
   breasts
2 tblsp. cooking oil
2 tblsp. sesame oil
1 lb. fresh green beans,
   cut into 2″ diagonal
   slices
2 cloves garlic, minced
4 chicken bouillon cubes,
   crumbled

3 tblsp. soy sauce
2 c. water
¼ c. sliced green onions
8 tsp. cornstarch
⅓ c. water
Hot cooked rice
Chow mein noodles

Cut and measure all ingredients before starting to cook.

Remove skin and bones from chicken. Cut into $2\frac{1}{2} \times \frac{3}{8}$″ strips.

Heat 1 tblsp. of the cooking oil and 1 tblsp. of the sesame oil in 12″ skillet or electric frypan over medium heat (325⁰) 5 minutes.

Add chicken and stir-fry 3 minutes or until chicken becomes opaque. Remove chicken from skillet.

Add remaining 1 tblsp. cooking oil and 1 tblsp. sesame oil to skillet and heat 1 minute. Add green beans and garlic. Stir-fry 1 minute. Add chicken bouillon cubes, soy sauce and 2 c. water. Cook until mixture comes to a boil, about 4 minutes. Reduce heat to low (220⁰). Cover and cook 10 minutes or until beans are tender-crisp, stirring occasionally.

Uncover and increase heat to medium (325⁰). Stir in chicken and green onions. Combine cornstarch and ⅓ c. water in small bowl; stir until blended. Stir into vegetable mixture. Bring to a boil, stirring constantly, about 1 minute. Boil 1 minute. Serve with rice and sprinkle with chow mein noodles.

Makes 4 servings.

85/Chicken fried rice

• *Preparation time: 18 minutes*
• *Cooking time: 13 minutes*

"I usually use leftover pork or chicken in this fried rice recipe. Just add it with the rice and heat," wrote a Virginia farm wife.

1 (1-lb.) whole chicken
   breast
3 tblsp. cooking oil
2 eggs
1 c. chopped onion
1 clove garlic, minced
1 (16-oz.) can bean
   sprouts, drained
1 (4-oz.) can mushroom
   stems and pieces,
   drained

3 c. cooked regular rice
1 (10-oz.) pkg. frozen peas,
   thawed
½ c. sliced green onions
4 tblsp. soy sauce
¼ tsp. ground ginger

Cut and measure all ingredients before starting to cook.

Remove skin and bones from chicken. Cut into 1″ cubes.

Heat 2 tblsp. of the oil in 12″ skillet or electric frypan over medium heat (300⁰) 5 minutes.

Beat eggs in bowl with rotary beater until blended. Add to hot oil. Cook 1 minute, stirring frequently, until eggs are set. Remove eggs from skillet and set aside.

Add remaining 1 tblsp. oil to skillet. Increase heat to medium-high (350⁰). Heat oil 2 minutes.

Add chicken, onion and garlic. Stir-fry 2 minutes or until chicken becomes opaque. Add bean sprouts and mushrooms. Stir-fry 1 minute.

Stir in rice, peas, green onions, soy sauce and ginger. Reduce heat to low (220⁰). Cover and simmer 2 minutes or until peas are tender.

Cut up cooked egg. Stir into rice mixture.

Makes 6 servings.

86/Sweet-and-sour turkey

- *Preparation time: 15 minutes*
- *Cooking time: 15 minutes*

This recipe transforms leftover turkey into an attractive main dish that's suitable for the most finicky dinner guests. So easy, too!

1 (20-oz.) can pineapple
  chunks in juice
Water
½ c. brown sugar, packed
¼ c. cornstarch
½ tsp. ground ginger
½ c. cider vinegar

¼ c. soy sauce
1¼ c. green pepper strips
1 c. sliced onion
1 c. sliced pared carrots
2 c. cubed cooked turkey
Hot cooked rice

Cut and measure all ingredients before starting to cook.

Drain pineapple, reserving juice. Add enough water to juice to make 2½ c. Combine brown sugar, cornstarch and ginger in 12″ skillet or electric frypan. Gradually stir in 2½ c. liquid, vinegar and soy sauce.

Place over high heat (400⁰). Cook until mixture comes to a boil, stirring constantly, about 5 minutes. Add pineapple chunks, green pepper, onion, carrots and turkey. Reduce heat to low (220⁰).

Cover and simmer 10 minutes or until vegetables are tender-crisp. Serve with rice.

Makes 6 servings.

FARM JOURNAL'S SPEEDY SKILLET MEALS

87/Shrimp with asparagus

• *Preparation time: 30 minutes*
• *Cooking time: 15 minutes*

Shrimp and asparagus make a lovely combination in this delicately sauced dish featuring chicken broth, sherry and soy sauce.

½ c. chicken broth
3 tblsp. dry sherry
1 tblsp. soy sauce
¼ tsp. sugar
1 tblsp. cornstarch
3 tblsp. sesame oil
1 clove garlic, minced

1 lb. fresh asparagus,
  bias-cut in ¼″ slices
3 tblsp. water
1 lb. medium shrimp,
  shelled and deveined
½ c. sliced green onions
Hot cooked rice

Cut and measure all ingredients before starting to cook.

Combine chicken broth, sherry, soy sauce, sugar and cornstarch in small bowl; stir to blend. Set aside.

Heat 2 tblsp. of the sesame oil in 12″ skillet or electric fry-pan over medium heat (325⁰) 5 minutes.

Add garlic and asparagus. Stir-fry 2 minutes. Add water. Cover and cook 3 minutes.

Add remaining 1 tblsp. sesame oil. Add shrimp and stir-fry 3 minutes or until asparagus is tender-crisp.

Stir cornstarch mixture and green onions into vegetable mixture. Cook, stirring constantly, until mixture comes to a boil, about 1 minute.

Boil 1 minute more. Serve with rice.

Makes 4 servings.

88/Shrimp egg foo yung

• *Preparation time: 4 minutes*
• *Cooking time: 39 minutes*

Makes a special luncheon when accompanied by a spinach and mushroom salad and a light dessert such as lemon sherbet.

6 eggs
1 (16-oz.) can Oriental mixed vegetables, well drained
½ c. thinly sliced green onions
1 (6-oz.) pkg. frozen cooked small shrimp, thawed
¼ tsp. salt

4 tblsp. cooking oil
2 tsp. cornstarch
1 tsp. sugar
¾ tsp. salt
½ c. water
1 tsp. vinegar
2 tsp. soy sauce
1 tblsp. sliced green onions

Cut and measure all ingredients before starting to cook.

Beat eggs in bowl with fork until blended. Stir in mixed vegetables, ½ c. green onions, shrimp and ¼ tsp. salt.

Heat 1 tsp. of the oil in 12″ skillet or electric frypan over medium heat (325⁰) 1 minute.

Add ¼ c. of the egg mixture to skillet. Flatten with a pancake turner to form a 5″ circle. Cook 1 minute and turn over. Cook 1 minute more or until golden brown. Remove from skillet and keep warm. Repeat with remaining egg mixture, adding 1 tsp. of the oil to skillet before cooking each one. (Total cooking time: 33 minutes.)

Combine cornstarch, sugar and ¾ tsp. salt in small saucepan. Stir in water, vinegar and soy sauce. Cook over medium heat, stirring constantly, until mixture boils and thickens, about 2 minutes. Boil 1 minute more. Stir in 1 tblsp. green onions. Remove from heat. Serve sauce with egg patties.

Makes 6 servings.

89/Oriental tuna

- *Preparation time: 15 minutes*
- *Cooking time: 14 minutes*

If you cut up the ingredients early in the day, you can actually cook this in 14 minutes. Start the rice before you begin to stir-fry.

2 tblsp. cornstarch
¼ tsp. ground ginger
1 (13¾-oz.) can chicken broth
3 tblsp. soy sauce
3 tblsp. cooking oil
1 c. bias-cut celery, ¼" slices
1 c. bias-cut pared carrots, ⅛" slices

1 clove garlic, minced
¼ c. sliced green onions
2 (7-oz.) cans water-pack tuna, drained and broken in chunks
1 (16-oz.) can bean sprouts, drained
1 c. frozen peas, thawed
Hot cooked rice

Cut and measure all ingredients before starting to cook.

Combine cornstarch, ginger, chicken broth and soy sauce in small bowl; stir to blend. Set aside.

Heat oil in 12" skillet or electric frypan over medium-high heat (375⁰) 5 minutes or until hot.

Add celery, carrots and garlic. Stir-fry 3 minutes. Add green onions and stir-fry 1 minute. Stir in cornstarch mixture. Cook, stirring constantly, until mixture boils and thickens, about 2 minutes.

Stir in tuna, bean sprouts and peas. Reduce heat to low (220⁰). Cover and simmer 3 minutes or until thoroughly heated. Serve with rice.

Makes 6 servings.

EASY STIR-FRIED DISHES

*90/*Oriental stir-fried vegetables

* *Preparation time: 20 minutes*
* *Cooking time: 16 minutes*

A tasty combination of exciting flavors and textures—toasted sesame seeds add a slightly nutty flavor. (See photo, Plate 1.)

1½ lb. fresh broccoli
3 tblsp. cooking oil
1 tblsp. sesame oil
½ tsp. salt
1 clove garlic, minced
1 c. chicken broth
1 (16-oz.) can bean
  sprouts, drained
1 (8-oz.) can water
  chestnuts, drained and
  sliced

¼ lb. fresh mushrooms,
  sliced
1 (6-oz.) pkg. frozen pea
  pods, thawed
2 tsp. cornstarch
1 tsp. sugar
⅛ tsp. ground ginger
1 tblsp. soy sauce
1 tblsp. toasted sesame
  seeds

Cut and measure all ingredients before starting to cook.

Remove flowerets from broccoli and cut in half. Cut stalks into 2 × ¼" strips.

Heat oil and sesame oil in 12" skillet or electric frypan over medium heat (325⁰) 5 minutes.

Add broccoli and stir-fry 1 minute. Add salt, garlic and ½ c. of the chicken broth. Cover and cook 3 minutes.

Uncover and stir-fry 3 minutes.

Add bean sprouts, water chestnuts, mushrooms and pea pods. Stir-fry 2 minutes.

Combine cornstarch, sugar, ginger, soy sauce and remaining ½ c. chicken broth; stir to blend. Stir cornstarch mixture into skillet. Cook until mixture comes to a boil, stirring constantly, about 1 minute. Boil 1 minute more. Sprinkle with sesame seeds before serving.

Makes 4 to 6 servings.

3 Family-style favorites

By far the most popular kinds of skillet recipes among country cooks are family-style dishes. Farm women specialize in serving fare that's nutritionally sound and has a rich home-cooked flavor.

Time is on their minds, too: They never seem to have enough time to spend in the kitchen, and we kept this in mind when we tested recipes for this section. Each recipe's preparation time is a half hour or less, although the cooking times vary from 17 minutes to 2½ hours.

This chapter contains 73 recipes well-suited to the average American's taste. Many of these are country favorites that have been converted to skillet cookery: Meat Loaf and Vegetables, a complete meal-in-a-skillet that consists of a tasty beef loaf surrounded with potatoes, carrot strips, diced zucchini and tomatoes; Scalloped Potatoes with Ham with a Cheddar cheese sauce and fresh green beans; and Barbecued Chicken with Peppers, which needs only six minutes' preparation time before cooking.

Quick-cooking seafood dishes are included, too. There's Landlubber's Seafood Chowder, a hearty combination of haddock, canned clams, cubed potatoes, sliced carrots and stewed tomatoes with a touch of rosemary and a sprinkle of parsley. Tuna Burgers with Noodles is a modified tuna casserole featuring tuna patties simmered with green beans and noodles in a dill-seasoned sour cream sauce.

Whichever recipes you choose, we hope they'll soon become family favorites at your house, too.

92/Pepper steak with potatoes

• *Preparation time: 29 minutes*
• *Cooking time: 1 hour 38 minutes*

A meat-and-potato lover's dream: extra-tender round steak simmered in lots of rich brown gravy and topped with pepper strips.

½ c. flour
½ tsp. salt
¼ tsp. pepper
2 lb. beef round steak, cut into serving pieces
¼ c. cooking oil
2 c. sliced onion
½ lb. fresh mushrooms, sliced
2 cloves garlic, minced
1 (16-oz.) can tomatoes, puréed in blender

2½ c. water
4 beef bouillon cubes
2 green peppers, cut into strips
2 tblsp. cornstarch
¼ c. water
1 tblsp. Worcestershire sauce
Hot mashed potatoes

Cut and measure all ingredients before starting to cook.

Combine flour, salt and pepper on a plate. Dredge beef in flour mixture.

Heat oil in 12″ skillet or electric frypan over medium heat (350⁰) 5 minutes or until hot. Brown beef on both sides in hot oil, about 10 minutes. Push beef to one side of skillet. Add onion, mushrooms and garlic. Sauté 10 minutes.

Stir in tomatoes, 2½ c. water and beef bouillon cubes. Cook until mixture comes to a boil, about 1 minute. Reduce heat to low (220⁰). Cover and simmer 1 hour or until meat is tender.

Add green pepper strips. Cover and simmer 10 minutes.

Remove meat to serving platter and keep warm.

Combine cornstarch and ¼ c. water in bowl; stir to blend. Stir into hot pan juices with Worcestershire sauce. Cook, stirring constantly, until mixture boils and thickens, about 2 minutes. Serve with meat and mashed potatoes.

Makes 6 to 8 servings.

93/Italian-seasoned steak

- *Preparation time: 30 minutes*
- *Cooking time: 1 hour 24 minutes*

Tomatoes, mushrooms and zucchini add interest to this steak dinner seasoned with oregano and basil.

2 lb. beef round steak,
  1" thick
¼ c. flour
½ tsp. salt
¼ tsp. pepper
3 tblsp. cooking oil
½ lb. fresh mushrooms,
  sliced
1 c. chopped onion
1 c. chopped green pepper
1 clove garlic, minced
1 (28-oz.) can tomatoes,
  cut up

1½ tsp. dried oregano
  leaves
1 tsp. dried basil leaves
1 lb. zucchini, cut into
  ¼" slices
Hot cooked wide noodles
1 tblsp. flour
2 tblsp. water
1 c. shredded mozzarella
  cheese

Cut and measure all ingredients before starting to cook.

Cut steak into serving pieces. Pound steak with meat mallet to tenderize. Combine ¼ c. flour, salt and pepper in pie plate. Dredge steak in flour mixture. Heat oil in 12" skillet or electric frypan over high heat (400⁰) 5 minutes or until hot.

Brown steak on both sides, about 10 minutes. Add mushrooms, onion, green pepper and garlic to skillet. Sauté 5 minutes.

Stir in tomatoes, oregano and basil. Cook until mixture comes to a boil, 1 minute. Reduce heat to low (220⁰). Cover and simmer 35 minutes. Add zucchini. Cover and simmer 25 minutes more or until meat is tender.

Arrange noodles on platter. Top with meat and keep warm. Combine 1 tblsp. flour and water in small jar. Cover and shake until blended. Stir into pan juices. Cook over high heat (400⁰), stirring constantly, until mixture boils and thickens, about 3 minutes. Pour over meat and top with mozzarella cheese.

Makes 6 servings.

94/Beef barbecue buns

- *Preparation time: 30 minutes*
- *Cooking time: 2 hours 31 minutes*

Tender slices of beef roast smothered in a tangy barbecue sauce make a meal for avid Sunday sports fans. (See photo, Plate 5.)

2 tblsp. cooking oil
2½ lb. boneless beef chuck
  roast
1 c. chopped onion
½ c. chopped green pepper
1 (14-oz.) bottle ketchup
2 tblsp. brown sugar,
  packed

2 tblsp. cider vinegar
1 tblsp. prepared yellow
  mustard
¼ c. water
16 hamburger buns, split

Cut and measure all ingredients before starting to cook.

Heat oil in 12″ skillet or electric frypan over medium heat (350⁰) 5 minutes or until hot.

Brown beef roast on all sides in hot oil, turning as needed, 10 minutes. Add onion and green pepper; sauté until tender, about 5 minutes.

Stir in ketchup, brown sugar, vinegar, mustard and water. Cook until mixture comes to a boil, about 1 minute.

Reduce heat to low (220⁰). Cover and simmer 2 hours or until meat is tender. Remove from heat.

Remove meat from skillet and place on cutting board. Cool slightly, about 15 minutes.

Thinly slice meat across the grain and return to skillet. Heat over low heat (220⁰) 10 minutes or until hot. Serve on hamburger buns.

Makes 16 servings.

95/**Stuffed beef rolls**

- *Preparation time: 20 minutes*
- *Cooking time: 50 minutes*

These easily made beef rolls filled with herb-seasoned stuffing cook in a spicy tomato sauce. Perfect with parslied potatoes.

1½ c. herb-seasoned stuffing mix	1 (1½-oz.) pkg. seasoning mix for Sloppy Joes
2 tblsp. butter or regular margarine, melted	1 (8-oz.) can tomato sauce
½ c. hot water	1 c. water
6 beef cube steaks (2 lb.)	1 tblsp. flour
2 tblsp. cooking oil	¼ c. water

Cut and measure all ingredients before starting to cook.

Combine stuffing mix, melted butter and ½ c. hot water in bowl. Mix lightly, but well. Spread stuffing mixture evenly over center of each cube steak. Roll up each steak like a jelly roll and fasten with toothpick or skewer.

Heat oil in 12″ skillet or electric frypan over medium heat (350⁰) 5 minutes or until hot.

Brown beef rolls in hot oil on all sides, about 10 minutes.

Combine seasoning mix, tomato sauce and 1 c. water in bowl; mix well. Pour over beef rolls. Cook until mixture comes to a boil, about 2 minutes.

Reduce heat to low (220⁰). Cover and simmer 30 minutes or until meat is tender.

Remove meat rolls to platter and keep warm. Combine flour and ¼ c. water in small jar. Cover and shake until blended. Stir flour mixture into skillet. Cook, stirring constantly, until mixture boils and thickens, about 3 minutes.

Makes 6 servings.

96/Vegetable dumpling soup

- *Preparation time: 20 minutes*
- *Cooking time: 59 minutes*

Soup makes a meal when it's as hearty as this one featuring tender beef cubes, a mix of vegetables and tender light dumplings.

2 tblsp. cooking oil
1 lb. beef chuck, cut into
  ½" cubes
¾ c. chopped onion
¾ c. thinly sliced pared
  carrots
¾ c. sliced celery, ⅛" thick
1 (8-oz.) can stewed
  tomatoes
7½ c. water

5 beef bouillon cubes
1 tsp. Worcestershire
  sauce
¼ tsp. pepper
2 tblsp. chopped fresh
  parsley
1 c. diced unpared
  zucchini
¾ c. buttermilk baking mix
¼ c. milk

Cut and measure all ingredients before starting to cook.

Heat oil in 12" skillet or electric frypan over medium heat (350°) 5 minutes or until hot.

Cook beef cubes 4 minutes or until browned. Add onion, carrots, celery, tomatoes, water, beef bouillon cubes, Worcestershire sauce, pepper and parsley. Cook until mixture comes to a boil, about 5 minutes.

Reduce heat to low (220°). Cover and simmer 30 minutes.

Add zucchini. Cover and simmer 10 minutes more.

Meanwhile, combine baking mix and milk in small bowl. Stir until blended. Drop dumpling mixture by teaspoonfuls into simmering soup. Cover and simmer 5 minutes more.

Makes 4 servings.

97/Spicy zucchini supper

• *Preparation time: 7 minutes*
• *Cooking time: 32 minutes*

Keep this skillet recipe handy for the zucchini season. It's extra-fast and such an interesting way to serve that prolific vegetable.

1 lb. ground beef	1 c. water
1 c. chopped onion	½ tsp. salt
½ c. chopped green pepper	⅛ tsp. pepper
1 (16-oz.) can tomatoes, cut up	1 c. raw quick-cooking rice
1 (1½-oz.) pkg. spaghetti sauce mix	4 c. sliced unpared zucchini
	Grated Parmesan cheese

Cut and measure all ingredients before starting to cook.

Cook ground beef, onion and green pepper in 12″ skillet or electric frypan over medium heat (350⁰) 5 minutes or until meat is browned.

Stir in tomatoes, spaghetti sauce mix, water, salt and pepper. Cook until mixture comes to a boil, about 2 minutes.

Stir in rice and zucchini. Reduce heat to low (220⁰). Cover and simmer 25 minutes or until zucchini and rice are tender.

Sprinkle with Parmesan cheese before serving.

Makes 6 servings.

FAMILY-STYLE FAVORITES

98/Miniature meat loaves

• *Preparation time: 25 minutes*
• *Cooking time: 50 minutes*

A complete family-style meal combining miniature parsley-flecked meat loaves, carrots and creamy mashed potato puffs.

1½ lb. ground chuck
1½ c. soft bread crumbs
½ c. chopped onion
¼ c. chopped fresh parsley
1 egg
1 c. milk
1 tsp. salt
1 small onion, cut into
  6 slices
3 c. water

2 tsp. beef bouillon
  granules
½ tsp. browning for gravy
2 (1½-oz.) pkg. mushroom
  gravy mix
3 c. sliced pared carrots
½ c. flour
1 c. water
4 c. hot mashed potatoes
Paprika

Cut and measure all ingredients before starting to cook.

Combine ground chuck, bread crumbs, ½ c. chopped onion, parsley, egg, milk and salt in bowl. Mix lightly, but well. Shape mixture into 6 small loaves and top each with an onion slice.

Heat 12″ skillet or electric frypan over low heat (220⁰) 5 minutes or until hot.

Place loaves into hot skillet. Cover and cook 15 minutes.

Remove loaves. Add 3 c. water, beef bouillon granules, browning for gravy, mushroom gravy mix and carrots to skillet. Cook over low heat (220⁰) until mixture comes to a boil, about 3 minutes. Meanwhile, combine flour and 1 c. water in small jar. Cover and shake until blended.

Stir flour mixture into skillet. Cook, stirring constantly, until mixture boils and thickens, about 2 minutes. Return meat loaves to skillet. Cover and simmer 20 minutes or until carrots are tender.

Spoon 12 puffs of mashed potatoes around edge of skillet. Sprinkle each puff with paprika. Cover and simmer 5 minutes more.

Makes 6 servings.

99/German skillet dinner

- *Preparation time: 5 minutes*
- *Cooking time: 36 minutes*

A treasured recipe brought to this country from Germany. It's been a favorite in one Wisconsin family for more than three generations.

2 tblsp. butter or regular margarine
1 lb. ground beef
1 c. chopped onion
1¼ tsp. salt
½ tsp. pepper

1 c. uncooked regular rice
2 (8-oz.) cans tomato sauce
1 (16-oz.) can sauerkraut
½ tsp. caraway seeds
1 c. water

Cut and measure all ingredients before starting to cook.

Melt butter in 10″ skillet over medium heat, about 2 minutes.

Cook ground beef, onion, salt and pepper 8 minutes or until well browned.

Stir in rice, tomato sauce, sauerkraut, caraway seeds and water. Cook until mixture comes to a boil, about 1 minute.

Reduce heat to low. Cover and simmer 25 minutes or until rice is tender.

Makes 6 servings.

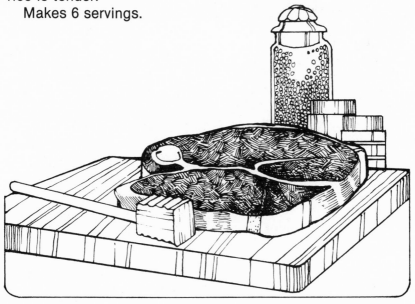

100/Summer meatball stew

• Preparation time: 28 minutes
• Cooking time: 1 hour

A light supper dish well suited to warm summer weather. Team it with a cool gelatin salad and golden brown Parker House rolls.

1 lb. ground chuck
½ c. soft bread crumbs
¼ c. chopped fresh parsley
1 egg
¼ c. milk
¾ tsp. salt
½ tsp. dried oregano leaves
¼ tsp. pepper
2 tblsp. cooking oil
½ lb. fresh mushrooms, sliced
1½ c. green pepper strips

1 c. chopped onion
1 clove garlic, minced
½ lb. fresh green beans, cut into 2″ pieces
1 (28-oz.) can tomatoes, cut up
1 beef bouillon cube
2 c. water
1 tsp. dried oregano leaves
½ tsp. dried basil leaves
1 lb. zucchini, sliced

Cut and measure all ingredients before starting to cook.

Combine ground chuck, bread crumbs, parsley, egg, milk, salt, ½ tsp. oregano and pepper in bowl. Mix lightly, but well. Shape mixture into 24 meatballs.

Heat oil in 12″ skillet or electric frypan over medium heat (300°) 5 minutes or until hot.

Brown meatballs, about 8 minutes. Remove meatballs from skillet. Add mushrooms, green pepper, onion and garlic to skillet. Sauté 10 minutes or until tender. Pour off excess fat.

Stir in meatballs, green beans, tomatoes, beef bouillon cube, water, 1 tsp. oregano and basil. Cook until mixture comes to a boil, about 2 minutes.

Reduce heat to low (220°). Cover and simmer 15 minutes.

Add zucchini. Cover and simmer 20 minutes more or until vegetables are tender.

Makes 8 servings.

101/Stuffed cabbage rolls

- *Preparation time: 25 minutes*
- *Cooking time: 1 hour 5 minutes*

"I'd like to share this recipe with other families. It's inexpensive to fix, easy and quick!" an Iowa homemaker told us.

1 large head cabbage	1 (28-oz.) can tomatoes,
Boiling water	cut up
1 lb. ground chuck	1 (8-oz.) can tomato sauce
1 c. cooked regular rice	¼ tsp. dried thyme leaves
⅓ c. finely chopped onion	¼ tsp. salt
¼ c. chopped fresh parsley	5 tsp. cornstarch
¼ tsp. dried thyme leaves	3 tblsp. water
1 tsp. salt	Fresh parsley sprigs
⅛ tsp. pepper	

Remove 10 large outside leaves from cabbage. Cut out coarse vein from each leaf. Place leaves in a large bowl and cover with boiling water. Let stand 15 minutes or until leaves are limp.

Cut and measure remaining ingredients. Drain off water and pat cabbage leaves dry with a paper towel.

Combine ground chuck, cooked rice, onion, ¼ c. parsley, ¼ tsp. thyme, 1 tsp. salt, pepper and 1½ c. of the tomatoes in bowl. Mix lightly, but well. Place an equal portion of the meat mixture in center of each cabbage leaf. Fold leaf over meat mixture on two sides and roll up gently. Secure end with toothpick. Place cabbage rolls in 12″ skillet or electric frypan.

Combine remaining tomatoes, tomato sauce, ¼ tsp. thyme and ¼ tsp. salt. Pour over cabbage rolls. Place over medium heat (350⁰) and cook until it comes to a boil, about 2 minutes. Reduce heat to low (220⁰). Cover and simmer 1 hour or until rolls are tender. Remove cabbage rolls to platter.

Combine cornstarch and 3 tblsp. water in small bowl; stir to blend. Stir into skillet. Cook over medium heat (350⁰), stirring constantly, until mixture boils and thickens, about 3 minutes. Pour over cabbage rolls and sprinkle with parsley .

Makes 5 servings.

102/Meat loaf and vegetables

- *Preparation time: 12 minutes*
- *Cooking time: 1 hour 20 minutes*

A complete meal including meat loaf, potatoes and carrots in a tomato-enriched gravy—and it's all cooked in a skillet.

1 lb. ground chuck
⅓ c. soft bread crumbs
1 egg, slightly beaten
½ tsp. salt
⅛ tsp. pepper
1 tblsp. cooking oil
1 (8-oz.) can tomato sauce
4 small potatoes, pared
  and quartered

4 medium carrots, pared
  and cut into 3″ strips
1 c. beef broth
¼ tsp. dried basil leaves
1 lb. zucchini, diced
½ tsp. salt
1 tblsp. cornstarch
2 tblsp. water

Cut and measure all ingredients before starting to cook.

Combine ground chuck, bread crumbs, egg, ½ tsp. salt and pepper in bowl. Mix lightly, but well. Shape mixture into a 6 × 4″ oval loaf. Heat oil in 12″ skillet or electric frypan over medium-high heat (375⁰) 5 minutes or until hot.

Brown meat loaf on all sides, about 6 minutes.

Spread 3 tblsp. of the tomato sauce on top of meat loaf. Arrange potatoes and carrots around loaf. Combine remaining tomato sauce with beef broth and basil. Pour over vegetables. Cook until it comes to a boil, about 2 minutes.

Reduce heat to low (220⁰). Cover and simmer 30 minutes.

Add zucchini and sprinkle with ½ tsp. salt. Cover and simmer 35 minutes or until vegetables are tender.

Arrange meat loaf and vegetables on a platter and keep warm. Combine cornstarch and water in small bowl; stir to blend. Stir cornstarch mixture into pan juices. Cook over medium heat (350⁰), stirring constantly, until mixture boils and thickens, about 2 minutes. Serve gravy with meat loaf and vegetables.

Makes 4 servings.

103/Cheese-stuffed peppers

• *Preparation time: 9 minutes*
• *Cooking time: 53 minutes*

Green pepper halves stuffed with a ground beef filling featuring rice and Cheddar cheese and simmered in a stewed tomato gravy.

3 c. water
½ tsp. salt
3 large green peppers, seeded and cut into lengthwise halves
1 (10¾-oz.) can condensed tomato soup
1 (16-oz.) can stewed tomatoes
½ tsp. celery seeds
2 drops Tabasco sauce

1 lb. ground chuck
½ c. chopped onion
1 clove garlic, minced
½ tsp. salt
⅛ tsp. pepper
2 tsp. Worcestershire sauce
1½ c. cooked regular rice
1 c. shredded Cheddar cheese

Cut and measure all ingredients before starting to cook.

Combine water and ½ tsp. salt in 12″ skillet or electric frypan over high heat (400⁰). Cook until mixture comes to a boil, about 3 minutes. Add green pepper halves. Cover and cook 5 minutes. Remove peppers and drain water from skillet.

Combine tomato soup, stewed tomatoes, celery seeds and Tabasco sauce in bowl; set aside.

Cook ground chuck, onion and garlic in same skillet over medium-high heat (375⁰) 12 minutes or until well browned.

Remove from heat. Stir in salt, pepper, Worcestershire sauce, rice, cheese and one-half of the tomato mixture. Mix well. Fill each pepper half with about ½ c. of meat mixture. Rinse out skillet.

Arrange stuffed peppers in skillet. Pour remaining tomato mixture into skillet. Cook over medium heat (350⁰) until mixture comes to a boil, about 3 minutes. Reduce heat to low (220⁰). Cover and simmer 30 minutes or until peppers are tender.

Makes 6 servings.

104/Upside-down hamburger skillet

- *Preparation time: 19 minutes*
- *Cooking time: 36 minutes*

A novel skillet idea for a family supper...a layer of corn bread topped with a ring of ground beef filled with succotash.

Corn Bread Topping
  (recipe follows)
¾ c. water
¼ tsp. salt
1 (10-oz.) pkg. frozen
  succotash
¼ c. sliced ripe olives

1 lb. ground chuck
¾ c. chopped onion
1 clove garlic, minced
½ c. ketchup
½ tsp. dried thyme leaves
½ tsp. salt

Cut and measure all ingredients before starting to cook.
Prepare Corn Bread Topping and set aside.

Heat water and ¼ tsp. salt in 10″ skillet over high heat until it comes to a boil, about 2 minutes. Add succotash and return to a boil, about 2 minutes. Reduce heat to low and simmer, uncovered, 5 minutes. Remove from heat and turn into a bowl. (Do not drain.) Add olives. Wipe out skillet.

Cook ground chuck, onion and garlic in same skillet over medium-high heat 5 minutes or until browned. Drain off excess fat. Stir in ketchup, thyme and ½ tsp. salt. Push meat mixture to sides of skillet, forming a ring. Pour succotash with liquid into center of ring. Cook until mixture comes to a boil, about 2 minutes.

Pour Corn Bread Topping evenly over all. Reduce heat to low. Cover and simmer 20 minutes or until corn bread tests done. Remove from heat. Remove cover and let stand 5 minutes. Loosen edges and invert on serving plate.

Makes 6 servings.

Corn Bread Topping: Combine 1 c. yellow corn meal, 1 c. sifted flour, 4 tsp. baking powder, ½ tsp. salt, ¼ c. brown sugar (packed) and ½ c. shredded Cheddar cheese in bowl. Add 1 c. milk, ¼ c. cooking oil and 1 egg (beaten). Stir until moistened.

105/Family-style stroganoff

- *Preparation time: 6 minutes*
- *Cooking time: 32 minutes*

"My family likes this because it's so tasty and I like it because it's so easy to fix," a Kansas farm woman recently told us.

1 lb. ground chuck
1 c. chopped onion
1 c. dairy sour cream
2½ c. tomato juice
2 tsp. Worcestershire
  sauce
1 tsp. salt

⅛ tsp. pepper
⅛ tsp. celery salt
⅛ tsp. garlic powder
6 oz. uncooked medium
  noodles (3½ c.)
Chopped fresh parsley

Cut and measure all ingredients before starting to cook.

Cook ground chuck and onion in 10″ skillet over medium-high heat 10 minutes or until browned.

Combine sour cream, tomato juice, Worcestershire sauce, salt, pepper, celery salt and garlic powder in bowl; mix to blend.

Arrange noodles in a layer on top of browned beef mixture. Pour sour cream mixture evenly over noodles. Do not stir. Cook until mixture comes to a boil, about 2 minutes.

Reduce heat to low. Cover and simmer 20 minutes or until noodles are tender. Sprinkle with parsley before serving.

Makes 4 to 6 servings.

FAMILY-STYLE FAVORITES

106/Mozzarella meatball sandwiches

• *Preparation time: 15 minutes*
• *Cooking time: 22 minutes*

A Minnesota farm woman shared her recipe for pizza meatballs with us. We tried them on Italian rolls—they made a great sandwich.

1 lb. ground chuck
¼ c. chopped onion
1 egg, slightly beaten
½ tsp. salt
¼ tsp. pepper
16 cubes mozzarella
   cheese (½")
2 tblsp. cooking oil

¾ c. ketchup
1 (4-oz.) can mushroom
   stems and pieces
½ tsp. dried Italian
   seasoning
1 clove garlic, minced
4 (10") Italian rolls, split

Cut and measure all ingredients before starting to cook.

Combine ground chuck, onion, egg, salt and pepper in bowl. Mix lightly, but well. Shape mixture into 16 meatballs, placing a cheese cube in the center of each.

Heat oil in 10" skillet over medium-high heat 2 minutes or until hot.

Brown meatballs in hot oil on all sides, about 8 minutes. Remove meatballs from skillet and drain on paper towels. Drain off fat from skillet and wipe skillet with a paper towel.

Combine ketchup, undrained mushrooms, Italian seasoning and garlic in skillet; mix well. Add meatballs. Cook over medium-high heat until mixture comes to a boil, about 2 minutes.

Reduce heat to low. Cover and simmer 10 minutes.

Spoon meatballs with sauce into Italian rolls, using 4 meatballs per sandwich.

Makes 4 servings.

107/Beef and macaroni

• *Preparation time: 14 minutes*
• *Cooking time: 36 minutes*

Almost every farm family has its own concoction of this ground beef, tomato and macaroni dinner. This one has two cheeses.

1 lb. ground chuck
½ c. chopped onion
½ c. chopped celery
¼ c. chopped green pepper
1 (28-oz.) can tomatoes, cut up
½ c. water
1 beef bouillon cube
1 tsp. Worcestershire sauce
1 tsp. salt
¼ tsp. pepper
1 c. uncooked elbow macaroni
½ c. grated Parmesan cheese
¾ c. shredded Cheddar cheese

Cut and measure all ingredients before starting to cook.

Cook ground chuck, onion, celery and green pepper in 10″ skillet over medium-high heat 10 minutes or until browned.

Stir in tomatoes, water, beef bouillon cube, Worcestershire sauce, salt, pepper and macaroni. Cook until mixture comes to a boil, about 1 minute.

Reduce heat to low. Cover and simmer 25 minutes, stirring occasionally, or until macaroni is tender.

Stir in Parmesan cheese. Remove from heat. Sprinkle with Cheddar cheese. Cover and let stand 2 minutes.

Makes 4 to 6 servings.

108/Harvest-time stew

• Preparation time: 18 minutes
• Cooking time: 1 hour 17 minutes

Good hearty fare for campsite cooking or a harvest-time supper. It can be completely cooked a day ahead of time and reheated.

2 lb. ground chuck
½ c. chopped onion
1 clove garlic, minced
1 tblsp. dried parsley
  flakes
2 tsp. salt
1 tsp. dried basil leaves
½ tsp. pepper

1 (28-oz.) can tomatoes,
  cut up
4 c. cubed pared potatoes
  (¾")
1 (16-oz.) can pork and
  beans in tomato sauce
1 (10-oz.) pkg. frozen peas

Cut and measure all ingredients before starting to cook.

Heat 12" skillet or electric frypan over medium heat (350⁰) 5 minutes or until hot.

Cook ground chuck, onion and garlic in hot skillet until meat is browned, about 7 minutes. Pour off excess fat. Add parsley flakes, salt, basil and pepper.

Stir in tomatoes. Reduce heat to low (220⁰). Cover and simmer 35 minutes, stirring occasionally.

Add potatoes and pork and beans. Cover and simmer 20 minutes, stirring occasionally.

Add peas. Cover and simmer 10 minutes, stirring occasionally.

Makes 8 servings.

109/Cheesy beef with rice

• *Preparation time: 9 minutes*
• *Cooking time: 46 minutes*

Another one of those handy recipes to keep in your file when you need a meal in a hurry. Just keep the basics on hand.

1½ lb. ground chuck
1 c. chopped onion
1 clove garlic, minced
½ tsp. salt
¼ tsp. dried basil leaves
¼ tsp. dried oregano
  leaves
⅛ tsp. pepper
½ bay leaf
1 (10¾-oz.) can condensed
  golden mushroom soup

1 (28-oz.) can tomatoes,
  cut up
½ c. uncooked regular rice
2 slices yellow process
  American cheese, cut in
  half diagonally
2 slices white process
  American cheese, cut in
  half diagonally
¼ c. sliced pimiento-
  stuffed olives

Cut and measure all ingredients before starting to cook.

Cook ground chuck, onion and garlic in 10″ skillet over medium-high heat 10 minutes or until well browned.

Drain off excess fat. Add salt, basil, oregano, pepper and bay leaf. Stir in mushroom soup, tomatoes and rice. Cook until mixture comes to a boil, about 4 minutes. Reduce heat to low. Cover and simmer 30 minutes, stirring occasionally.

Arrange cheese triangles, pinwheel fashion, on top of meat mixture. Sprinkle with olives. Heat 2 minutes more or until cheese melts.

Makes 6 servings.

110/Gardener's skillet supper

- *Preparation time: 20 minutes*
- *Cooking time: 35 minutes*

You don't need to skimp on nutrition just because you're watching the budget. Here's a vegetable combination that's sure to please.

3 strips bacon
1 lb. ground beef
1 c. sliced onion
1 (16-oz.) can tomatoes, cut up
½ c. water
1 tsp. salt
¼ tsp. pepper

1 tblsp. Worcestershire sauce
2 medium potatoes, pared and diced
1 c. green pepper strips
2 c. coarsely chopped cabbage
1 c. chopped celery

Cut and measure all ingredients before starting to cook.

Fry bacon in 10″ skillet over medium heat 5 minutes or until crisp. Remove and drain on paper towels. Crumble bacon.

Pour off all but 2 tblsp. bacon drippings. Add ground beef and onion to bacon drippings. Cook over medium heat 8 minutes or until well browned.

Add tomatoes, water, salt, pepper, Worcestershire sauce, potatoes, green pepper, cabbage, celery and crumbled bacon. Cook until mixture comes to a boil, about 2 minutes.

Reduce heat to low. Cover and simmer 20 minutes or until vegetables are tender.

Makes 4 to 5 servings.

111/Hurry-up beef and potatoes

• Preparation time: 10 minutes
• Cooking time: 48 minutes

Just the kind of supper dish most farm women rely on during the extra-busy planting and harvesting seasons. Speedy and delicious!

3 c. sliced, pared potatoes
  (1 lb.)
½ tsp. salt
1 c. water
1 lb. ground chuck
1 c. sliced onion
1 (10¾-oz.) can condensed
  cream of celery soup

⅓ c. milk
1 c. shredded Cheddar
  cheese
⅛ tsp. pepper
Paprika

Cut and measure all ingredients before starting to cook.

Cook potatoes, salt and water in 10" skillet over high heat 2 minutes or until it comes to a boil. Reduce heat to low. Cover and simmer 10 minutes.

Remove from heat. Drain potatoes in colander.

Cook ground chuck and onion in same skillet over medium heat 10 minutes or until browned.

Stir in celery soup, milk, ¾ c. of the cheese and pepper. Reduce heat to low. Cook and stir until cheese is melted, about 1 minute. Remove meat sauce from skillet and place in bowl. Rinse out skillet.

Spoon 1 c. of the meat sauce into same skillet. Arrange one half of potatoes on top. Spoon 1 c. of the meat sauce over potatoes. Layer with remaining potatoes and top with remaining meat sauce. Cover and cook over low heat 20 minutes or until thoroughly heated.

Sprinkle with remaining ¼ c. cheese and paprika. Cover and cook 5 minutes more or until cheese melts.

Makes 4 servings.

112/Four-layer skillet dinner

• *Preparation time: 26 minutes*
• *Cooking time: 50 minutes*

"We like this because the vegetables don't lose their individual taste and yet the flavors mingle," wrote a South Dakota woman.

1 lb. ground chuck	1½ tsp. salt
1 c. chopped onion	⅛ tsp. pepper
6 medium potatoes, pared	1 (10-oz.) pkg. frozen peas
and sliced (2 lb.)	1 (16-oz.) can tomatoes,
2 c. milk	drained and cut in half
2 c. sliced pared carrots	½ c. green pepper strips
1 c. chopped celery	

Cut and measure all ingredients before starting to cook.

Cook ground chuck and onion in 12″ skillet or electric frypan over medium heat (350⁰) 10 minutes or until browned.

Remove from heat. Place meat mixture in bowl and set aside.

Spread potatoes in bottom of same skillet. Pour milk over potatoes. Top with meat mixture, then carrots and celery. Sprinkle with salt and pepper. Place over medium heat (350⁰) and cook until mixture comes to a boil, about 5 minutes.

Reduce heat to low (220⁰). Cover and simmer 25 minutes.

Arrange peas on top of mixture. Place tomatoes and green pepper strips alternately around edge of skillet. Cover and simmer 10 minutes more.

Makes 6 servings.

113/Barbecued beef sandwiches

- *Preparation time: 7 minutes*
- *Cooking time: 41 minutes*

Makes a good hot sandwich for a casual party or a special meeting. Cook it a day in advance and reheat—the flavor just gets better.

2 lb. ground chuck
1 c. chopped onion
1 c. chopped green pepper
2 (8-oz.) cans tomato
   sauce
1 (6-oz.) can tomato paste
2 tblsp. brown sugar,
   packed

3 tblsp. cider vinegar
2 tblsp. Worcestershire
   sauce
1 c. water
¼ tsp. salt
⅛ tsp. pepper
10 hamburger buns, split

Cut and measure all ingredients before starting to cook.

Cook ground chuck, onion and green pepper in 12″ skillet or electric frypan over medium heat (350⁰) 10 minutes or until browned.

Pour off fat from skillet. Stir in tomato sauce, tomato paste, brown sugar, vinegar, Worcestershire sauce, water, salt and pepper. Cook until mixture comes to a boil, about 1 minute.

Reduce heat to low (220⁰). Cover and simmer 30 minutes.

Spoon meat mixture onto bottom half of hamburger buns, using about ½ c. per bun. Cover with top half of buns.

Makes 10 servings.

114/Monterey chili con carne

• *Preparation time: 8 minutes*
• *Cooking time: 1 hour 7 minutes*

This recipe gets its name from the cheese used in it. Monterey Jack is a mild variety that melts easily. Longhorn is a good substitute.

1 lb. ground beef
1 c. chopped onion
1 clove garlic, minced
1 (28-oz.) can tomatoes, cut up
2 (15-oz.) cans red kidney beans

3 tsp. chili powder
1½ tsp. salt
1 tsp. ground cumin
¾ c. cubed Monterey Jack cheese (¼")

Cut and measure all ingredients before starting to cook.

Cook ground beef, onion and garlic in 12" skillet or electric frypan over high heat (400⁰) 5 minutes or until meat is browned. Drain off excess fat from skillet.

Stir in tomatoes, undrained kidney beans, chili powder, salt and cumin. Cook until mixture comes to a boil, about 2 minutes.

Reduce heat to low (220⁰). Cover and simmer 1 hour.

Sprinkle with Monterey Jack cheese before serving.

Makes 6 servings.

115/Midwestern-style chili

• *Preparation time: 10 minutes*
• *Cooking time: 1 hour 29 minutes*

A mildly seasoned chili that's extra-thick with elbow macaroni, onion, green pepper, celery and kidney beans. Serve with crackers.

6 c. water
½ tsp. salt
1½ c. uncooked elbow macaroni
1½ lb. ground chuck
1 c. chopped onion
½ c. chopped green pepper
½ c. chopped celery
2 cloves garlic, minced
1 (10½-oz.) can condensed onion soup

1 (10¾-oz.) can condensed tomato soup
1 (28-oz.) can tomatoes, cut up
¼ c. chopped fresh parsley
1 tblsp. chili powder
2 (15-oz.) cans red kidney beans

Cut and measure all ingredients before starting to cook.

Heat 6 c. water and salt in 12″ skillet or electric frypan over high heat (420⁰) 5 minutes or until it comes to a boil.

Add macaroni. Boil 8 minutes, stirring occasionally. Drain macaroni in colander and rinse with cold water. Wipe out skillet.

Cook ground chuck, onion, green pepper, celery and garlic in same skillet over medium-high heat (375⁰) 8 minutes or until well browned. Drain off excess fat.

Stir in onion soup, tomato soup, tomatoes, parsley and chili powder. Cook until mixture comes to a boil, about 3 minutes. Reduce heat to low (220⁰). Simmer, uncovered, 45 minutes, stirring occasionally.

Stir in undrained kidney beans. Simmer 15 minutes more.

Add macaroni and heat 5 minutes.

Makes 6 to 8 servings.

116/Chili with tacos

• *Preparation time: 8 minutes*
• *Cooking time: 41 minutes*

Easy-to-prepare chili con carne featuring green pepper, corn, beef and tomatoes—garnished with a ring of crunchy taco chips.

1 lb. ground chuck	1 c. uncooked elbow
½ c. chopped onion	macaroni
½ c. chopped green pepper	1 c. water
1 clove garlic, minced	1 tblsp. chili powder
2 (8-oz.) cans tomato	½ tsp. ground cumin
sauce	½ tsp. salt
1 (16-oz.) can tomatoes,	¼ tsp. pepper
cut up	Taco chips
1 (10-oz.) pkg. frozen corn	

Cut and measure all ingredients before starting to cook.

Cook ground chuck, onion, green pepper and garlic in 12″ skillet or electric frypan over medium heat (350⁰) 8 minutes or until well browned.

Stir in tomato sauce, tomatoes, corn, macaroni, water, chili powder, cumin, salt and pepper. Cook until mixture comes to a boil, about 3 minutes. Reduce heat to low (220⁰). Cover and simmer 30 minutes or until macaroni is tender.

Before serving, garnish inside edge of skillet with taco chips.

Makes 4 to 6 servings.

117/Basic beef and noodles

- *Preparation time: 15 minutes*
- *Cooking time: 42 minutes*

Sour cream and cottage cheese add a different flavor note to this basic noodle and beef dinner. Melted Cheddar cheese is the topper.

5 c. water
½ tsp. salt
8 oz. uncooked medium noodles
1 lb. ground chuck
¼ c. minced onion
1 clove garlic, minced
2 (8-oz.) cans tomato sauce

1 tsp. salt
¼ tsp. pepper
1 c. dairy sour cream
1 c. creamed small-curd cottage cheese
1 c. sliced cooked carrots
¼ c. chopped fresh parsley
1 c. shredded Cheddar cheese

Cut and measure all ingredients before starting to cook.

Heat water and ½ tsp. salt in 12" skillet or electric frypan over high heat (400°) 5 minutes or until it comes to a boil. Add noodles. Cover and cook 7 minutes or until tender, stirring occasionally.

Drain noodles in colander. Rinse with cold water; set aside.

Cook ground chuck, onion and garlic in same skillet over medium heat (350°) until browned, about 15 minutes. Stir in tomato sauce, 1 tsp. salt and pepper. Reduce heat to low (220°). Simmer 5 minutes.

Stir in noodles, sour cream, cottage cheese, carrots and parsley. Cover and simmer 8 minutes or until thoroughly heated.

Sprinkle with Cheddar cheese. Cover and simmer 2 minutes more or until cheese melts.

Makes 6 to 8 servings.

118/Home-style hamburgers

- *Preparation time: 18 minutes*
- *Cooking time: 43 minutes*

A good home-style meal made with plump hamburgers, cubed potatoes and carrot strips in a creamy mushroom-tomato gravy.

6 strips bacon
1½ lb. ground chuck
½ c. soft bread crumbs
½ c. finely chopped onion
¼ c. chopped fresh parsley
1 egg
½ c. milk
¼ tsp. pepper
5 medium potatoes, pared
  and cut into 1″ cubes
5 medium carrots, pared
  and cut into 2″ strips

1 (28-oz.) can tomatoes,
  cut up
1 (10¾-oz.) can condensed
  golden mushroom soup
½ c. water
1 tsp. dried marjoram
  leaves
2 tblsp. flour
¼ c. water

Cut and measure all ingredients before starting to cook.

Cook bacon in 12″ skillet or electric frypan over medium heat (325⁰) until browned, about 6 minutes. Remove and drain on paper towels.

Combine ground chuck, bread crumbs, onion, parsley, egg, milk and pepper in bowl. Mix lightly, but well. Shape into 6 patties. Brown patties on both sides in hot bacon drippings over medium heat (325⁰), about 6 minutes. Remove patties. Pour off excess fat from skillet.

Crumble bacon. Stir bacon, potatoes, carrots, tomatoes, soup, ½ c. water and marjoram into skillet. Place patties on top. Cook over medium heat (325⁰) until it comes to a boil, about 2 minutes. Reduce heat to low (220⁰). Cover and simmer 25 minutes or until vegetables are tender.

Combine flour and ¼ c. water in jar. Cover and shake until blended. Stir into pan juices. Cook over medium heat (325⁰), stirring constantly, until mixture boils and thickens, about 4 minutes. Pour sauce over meat.

Makes 6 servings.

119/Spaghetti in a skillet

• Preparation time: 9 minutes
• Cooking time: 41 minutes

Even the spaghetti is cooked in the skillet when you prepare this easy and inexpensive main dish. Complete the meal with a salad.

1 lb. ground chuck
1 c. chopped onion
1 c. chopped green pepper
1 clove garlic, minced
1 (28-oz.) can tomatoes,
  cut up
3 c. water
8 oz. uncooked spaghetti,
  broken into pieces

1 (4-oz.) can mushroom
  stems and pieces,
  drained
1 (6-oz.) can tomato paste
1 tsp. dried oregano leaves
½ tsp. dried basil leaves
1 tsp. salt
¼ tsp. pepper
Grated Parmesan cheese

Cut and measure all ingredients before starting to cook.

Cook ground chuck, onion, green pepper and garlic in 12″ skillet or electric frypan over medium heat (350⁰) 10 minutes or until well browned.

Stir in tomatoes, water, spaghetti, mushrooms, tomato paste, oregano, basil, salt and pepper. Bring mixture to a boil, about 1 minute.

Reduce heat to low (220⁰). Cover and simmer 30 minutes, stirring occasionally, or until spaghetti is tender. Sprinkle with Parmesan cheese before serving.

Makes 6 servings.

120/Porcupine meatballs

• Preparation time: 10 minutes
• Cooking time: 47 minutes

There's no need to brown the meatballs in this family-style entrée. Such a timesaver! Garnish with fresh parsley if you wish.

1 lb. ground beef
¼ c. uncooked regular rice
¼ c. finely chopped onion
1 tsp. salt
⅛ tsp. pepper
1 egg

1 (10¾-oz.) can condensed
tomato soup
¾ c. water
1 tsp. Worcestershire
sauce

Cut and measure all ingredients before starting to cook.

Combine ground beef, rice, onion, salt, pepper and egg in bowl. Mix lightly, but well. Form mixture into 24 (1″) meatballs.

Combine soup, water and Worcestershire sauce in 12″ skillet or electric frypan. Set heat at low (220⁰) and heat, about 2 minutes.

Add meatballs to simmering sauce, spooning sauce over meatballs. Cover and simmer 45 minutes, turning meatballs once or twice.

Makes 4 servings.

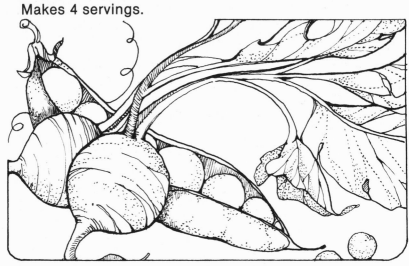

121/Beef liver in spicy sauce

- *Preparation time: 7 minutes*
- *Cooking time: 36 minutes*

Here's a different way to serve liver—in a tomato sauce seasoned with paprika, chili powder and Worcestershire over fluffy rice.

¼ c. flour
¼ c. brown sugar, packed
2 tsp. paprika
½ tsp. chili powder
¼ c. ketchup
1 (16-oz.) can stewed
  tomatoes, cut up
¼ c. cider vinegar

2 tblsp. Worcestershire
  sauce
1 lb. beef liver, sliced
3 tblsp. flour
3 tblsp. cooking oil
4 green pepper rings,
  ¼" thick
Hot cooked rice

Cut and measure all ingredients before starting to cook.

Blend together ¼ c. flour, brown sugar, paprika, chili powder, ketchup, tomatoes, vinegar and Worcestershire sauce in bowl; set aside.

Dredge beef liver in 3 tblsp. flour; set aside.

Heat oil in 10" skillet over medium-high heat 2 minutes or until hot.

Brown liver on both sides in hot oil, about 4 minutes.

Add tomato mixture to liver and top with pepper rings. Reduce heat to low. Cover and simmer 15 minutes.

Uncover and simmer 15 minutes more, stirring occasionally. Serve over hot cooked rice.

Makes 4 servings.

122/Upside-down corned beef hash

• *Preparation time: 8 minutes*
• *Cooking time: 30 minutes*

Canned corned beef hash and mixed vegetables make a nourishing meal when topped with corn bread. Invert on a plate to serve.

1 c. yellow corn meal
1 c. sifted flour
¼ c. brown sugar, packed
4 tsp. baking powder
½ tsp. salt
1 c. milk
¼ c. cooking oil
1 egg, beaten
¾ c. water

¼ tsp. salt
1 (10-oz.) pkg. frozen
 mixed vegetables
1 tblsp. cooking oil
2 tblsp. ketchup
1 tblsp. prepared yellow
 mustard
1 (15-oz.) can corned beef
 hash

Measure all ingredients before starting to cook.

Stir together corn meal, flour, brown sugar, baking powder and ½ tsp. salt in bowl. Combine milk, ¼ c. oil and egg in another bowl. Beat with rotary beater until blended. Set aside.

Combine water and ¼ tsp. salt in 10″ skillet over high heat. Cook until mixture comes to a boil, about 2 minutes. Add mixed vegetables and return to a boil, about 2 minutes. Reduce heat to low. Cover and simmer 3 minutes. Remove from heat and pour vegetables with cooking liquid into bowl.

Heat 1 tblsp. oil in same skillet over medium heat, about 1 minute. Combine ketchup and mustard with hash. Arrange hash mixture in a ring in skillet. Pour vegetables with liquid into center. Cook until it boils, about 2 minutes.

Pour liquid ingredients into corn meal mixture. Stir just until moistened. Pour corn meal mixture over hash and vegetables. Reduce heat to low. Cover; cook 20 minutes or until done. Remove from heat. Let stand, uncovered, 5 minutes. Loosen edges with spatula and invert on warm plate.

Makes 6 servings.

123/Hash and eggs

• Preparation time: 20 minutes
• Cooking time: 34 minutes

This is just the kind of supper dish that's perfect for a camping trip or an early morning breakfast before a hard day in the field.

¼ c. cooking oil	2 tblsp. ketchup
½ c. chopped onion	½ tsp. dry mustard
1 clove garlic, minced	⅛ tsp. pepper
3 c. diced cooked potatoes	6 eggs
1 (12-oz.) can corned beef, diced (2 c.)	3 slices process American cheese, cut in half diagonally
½ c. milk	

Cut and measure all ingredients before starting to cook.

Heat 2 tblsp. of the oil in 12″ skillet or electric frypan over medium heat (350⁰) 5 minutes or until hot.

Add onion and garlic. Sauté 3 minutes or until tender. Combine onion mixture with potatoes, corned beef, milk, ketchup, mustard and pepper in bowl. Mix lightly, but well.

Heat remaining 2 tblsp. oil in same skillet over medium heat (300⁰) 2 minutes or until hot.

Spread hash mixture in hot oil. Cook 5 minutes, turning occasionally with spatula.

Make 6 indentations in hash with back of a spoon. Break an egg into each indentation. Reduce heat to low (220⁰). Cover and cook 17 minutes or until eggs are set.

Place a half of a slice of cheese over each egg. Cover and cook 2 minutes more or until cheese is melted. Cut into 6 wedges.

Makes 6 servings.

124/Pork chops with stuffing

• Preparation time: 20 minutes
• Cooking time: 1 hour 25 minutes

This recipe resembles stuffed pork chops but it's so much easier. A mound of stuffing is placed on top of each chop.

½ c. butter or regular
  margarine
1 c. chopped onion
1 c. chopped celery
10 c. soft bread cubes
  (½")
2 tblsp. dried parsley
  flakes
½ tsp. salt
½ tsp. rubbed sage

½ tsp. pepper
½ c. hot water
3 tblsp. cooking oil
6 pork chops, ½" thick
Salt
Pepper
1 (10¾-oz.) can condensed
  cream of chicken soup
½ c. water

Cut and measure all ingredients before starting to cook.

Melt butter in 12" skillet or electric frypan over medium heat (350º), about 5 minutes.

Add onion and celery. Sauté 5 minutes or until tender. Remove from heat. Combine onion-celery mixture, bread cubes, parsley flakes, ½ tsp. salt, sage, ½ tsp. pepper and ½ c. hot water in large bowl. Mix lightly, but well. Set aside. Wipe out skillet.

Heat oil in same skillet or electric frypan over medium heat (350º) 5 minutes or until hot.

Season pork chops with salt and pepper. Brown pork chops on both sides in hot oil, about 10 minutes.

Form stuffing into 6 mounds and place on top of chops. Blend together soup and ½ c. water in bowl. Pour soup mixture over stuffing and chops.

Reduce heat to low (220º). Cover and simmer 1 hour or until pork chops are tender.

Makes 6 servings.

125/Pork chop skillet dinner

This popular Farm Journal recipe has been requested again and again. It's the perfect choice for a winter day. (See photo, Plate 2.)

1 tblsp. cooking oil
6 pork chops, ¾" thick
  (2½ lb.)
½ tsp. salt
¼ tsp. pepper
½ tsp. dried savory
  leaves
½ bay leaf
2 c. tomato juice
½ c. water

1 small cabbage, cut into
  6 wedges
6 carrots, pared and cut
  into 1" pieces
1½ c. coarsely chopped
  onion
3 medium potatoes, pared
  and quartered
¼ tsp. salt

Cut and measure all ingredients before starting to cook.

Heat oil in 12" skillet or electric frypan over medium-high heat (375⁰) 5 minutes or until hot.

Season pork chops with ½ tsp. salt and pepper. Brown pork chops on both sides in hot oil, about 10 minutes.

Add savory, bay leaf, tomato juice and water. Cook until mixture comes to a boil, about 3 minutes. Reduce heat to low (220⁰). Cover and simmer 30 minutes.

Add cabbage, carrots, onion, potatoes and ¼ tsp. salt. Cover and simmer 35 minutes more or until vegetables are tender.

Makes 6 servings.

126/Spanish-style pork chops

• Preparation time: 8 minutes
• Cooking time: 1 hour 3 minutes

All that's needed to complete this meal is a bowl of greens tossed with vinegar-oil dressing and fresh fruit with cheese for dessert.

1 tblsp. cooking oil
6 pork chops, ¾" thick
  (2½ lb.)
1 tsp. salt
⅛ tsp. pepper
1 (16-oz.) can tomatoes,
  cut up
½ c. chopped onion

½ c. chopped green
  pepper
½ c. chopped celery
¼ c. uncooked regular
  rice
2 tsp. dried parsley flakes
½ bay leaf
½ c. water

Cut and measure all ingredients before starting to cook.

Heat oil in 12″ skillet or electric frypan over medium-high heat (375⁰) 5 minutes or until hot.

Season pork chops with salt and pepper. Brown pork chops on both sides in hot oil, about 10 minutes.

Add tomatoes, onion, green pepper, celery, rice, parsley flakes, bay leaf and water to skillet. Cook until mixture comes to a boil, about 3 minutes.

Reduce heat to low (220⁰). Cover and simmer 45 minutes or until pork chops are tender.

Makes 6 servings.

127/Pork chops with kidney beans

• *Preparation time: 9 minutes*
• *Cooking time: 1 hour 4 minutes*

A simple, yet tasty dinner that really sticks to the ribs. Suitable for cold wintry days because it's such hearty fare.

**6 pork chops, ¾″ thick
(2½ lb.)
½ tsp. salt
⅛ tsp. pepper
½ c. chopped onion
2 (15½-oz.) cans red kidney
beans, drained
1 (6-oz.) can tomato paste**

**1 clove garlic, minced
1 tblsp. chili powder
3 c. water
1 green pepper, seeded
and cut into 6 rings
3 c. hot cooked rice
½ c. shredded Monterey
Jack cheese**

Cut and measure all ingredients before starting to cook.

Preheat 12″ skillet or electric frypan over medium heat (350⁰) 5 minutes or until hot.

Season pork chops with salt and pepper. Brown pork chops on both sides in hot skillet, about 10 minutes. Remove pork chops as they brown.

Add onion to skillet. Sauté 1 minute. Stir in kidney beans, tomato paste, garlic, chili powder and water. Arrange pork chops on top. Cook until mixture comes to a boil, about 3 minutes. Reduce heat to low (220⁰). Cover and simmer 30 minutes.

Place 1 green pepper ring on top of each chop. Cover and simmer 15 minutes more or until pork chops are tender.

Spoon beans into center of platter. Arrange rice in a ring around beans and place pork chops on top. Sprinkle with cheese.

Makes 6 servings.

128/Pork chops with corn

• *Preparation time: 6 minutes*
• *Cooking time: 1 hour 3 minutes*

This main dish is light and tasty. It's especially good with homemade baking powder biscuits and a fresh garden salad.

6 pork chops, ¾" thick
   (about 2½ lb.)
1 (13¾-oz.) can chicken
   broth
1 c. chopped green pepper
¼ c. finely chopped onion

2 (10-oz.) pkg. frozen
   whole-kernel corn
1 (4-oz.) jar sliced
   pimientos, drained
¼ tsp. cayenne pepper

Cut and measure all ingredients before starting to cook.

Preheat 12" skillet or electric frypan over medium heat (350⁰) 5 minutes or until hot.

Brown pork chops on both sides in hot skillet, about 10 minutes. Stir in chicken broth. Reduce heat to low (220⁰). Cover and simmer 30 minutes.

Stir in green pepper, onion, corn, pimientos and cayenne pepper. Cook until mixture comes to a boil, about 3 minutes. Cover and simmer 15 minutes more or until pork chops are tender.

Makes 6 servings.

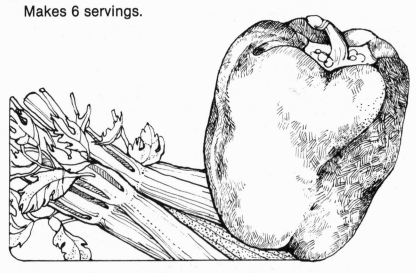

129/Hungarian pork with sauerkraut

- *Preparation time: 17 minutes*
- *Cooking time: 1 hour 35 minutes*

If you can find Hungarian paprika in an herb or spice shop, try it when you prepare this dish — it has more zip and flavor.

2 lb. boneless pork, cut
   into 1″ cubes
2 tblsp. cooking oil
2 (16-oz.) cans sauerkraut,
   drained and rinsed
½ c. chopped onion
1 clove garlic, minced

2 tsp. paprika
2 tsp. chicken bouillon
   granules
½ tsp. dried dillweed
1¼ c. water
½ c. dairy sour cream

Cut and measure all ingredients before starting to cook.

Trim excess fat from pork.

Heat oil in 12″ skillet or electric frypan over medium heat (350⁰) 5 minutes or until hot.

Cook pork in hot oil 10 minutes or until browned. Stir in sauerkraut, onion, garlic, paprika, chicken bouillon granules, dillweed and water. Cook until mixture comes to a boil, about 2 minutes.

Reduce heat to low (220⁰). Cover and simmer 1 hour 15 minutes or until pork is tender.

Stir some of hot mixture into sour cream. Then blend sour cream mixture into pork mixture. Heat 3 minutes (do not boil).

Makes 6 servings.

130/Candied sweet potatoes and ham patties

- *Preparation time: 18 minutes*
- *Cooking time: 33 minutes*

Ham patties topped with a ring of pineapple and a mound of orange-flavored sweet potatoes in a brown sugar sauce.

Mashed Sweet Potatoes
(recipe follows)
1½ lb. cooked ham, ground
¾ c. soft bread crumbs
½ c. chopped onion
2 tsp. yellow mustard
2 eggs

½ c. milk
⅛ tsp. pepper
½ c. butter or regular
margarine
2 (8-oz.) cans sliced pineapple in juice
¾ c. brown sugar, packed

Cut and measure all ingredients and prepare Mashed Sweet Potatoes before starting to cook.

Combine ground ham, bread crumbs, onion, mustard, eggs, milk and pepper in bowl and mix well. Shape mixture into 8 patties. Melt 2 tblsp. of the butter in 12″ skillet or electric frypan over medium-low heat (280⁰), about 1 minute.

Brown ham patties on both sides, about 6 minutes. Meanwhile, drain pineapple, reserving juice.

Remove ham patties from skillet. Stir remaining 6 tblsp. butter, brown sugar and 2 tblsp. of the pineapple juice into same skillet. Cook until mixture bubbles, about 4 minutes.

Add pineapple slices and cook 2 minutes, turning once. Place a pineapple slice on each patty and top with a mound of Mashed Sweet Potatoes. Stir ¼ c. pineapple juice into skillet. Arrange prepared patties in skillet. Reduce heat to low (220⁰). Cover and simmer 20 minutes. Arrange patties on platter. Simmer sauce 2 minutes. Spoon sauce over all.

Makes 8 servings.

Mashed Sweet Potatoes: Drain 2 (17-oz.) cans sweet potatoes. Rice sweet potatoes into bowl. Add ¼ c. orange juice, 2 tblsp. melted butter or regular margarine, 2 tsp. grated orange rind, 1 tsp. salt and ⅛ tsp. pepper; mix well.

131/Creamed ham with spinach and rice

• Preparation time: 20 minutes
• Cooking time: 32 minutes

If your children don't care for spinach, try serving it combined with ham and rice in an extra-cheesy cream sauce.

2 (10-oz.) pkg. fresh spinach	3 c. milk
4 tblsp. butter or regular margarine	1 lb. fully cooked ham steak, cut in 1″ cubes
¼ c. finely chopped onion	2 c. cooked regular rice
4 tblsp. flour	1 c. shredded Cheddar cheese
½ tsp. dry mustard	1 tblsp. prepared horseradish
¼ tsp. pepper	

Cut and measure all ingredients before starting to cook.

Wash spinach thoroughly and pinch off stems. Shake off excess water and chop coarsely.

Place spinach in 12″ skillet or electric frypan. Cover and place over medium heat (350⁰). Steam until wilted, about 5 minutes.

Remove spinach and drain in colander, pressing against sides to remove excess water. Set aside.

Melt butter in same skillet over medium heat (300⁰), about 2 minutes. Add onion and sauté 2 minutes. Blend in flour, mustard and pepper. Gradually stir in milk. Cook, stirring constantly, until mixture boils and thickens, about 12 minutes. Cook and stir 1 minute more.

Stir in drained spinach, ham, rice, cheese and horseradish. Cover and simmer over low heat (220⁰) 10 minutes or until thoroughly heated.

Makes 6 servings.

132/Ham and potato skillet

• *Preparation time: 38 minutes*
• *Cooking time: 54 minutes*

Peas, cubed potatoes and ham strips cook to perfection in this cheese sauce spiked with Worcestershire sauce and mustard.

5 c. water
2 lb. potatoes, pared and cut into 1″ cubes
¼ c. butter or regular margarine
¼ c. chopped onion
¼ c. flour
1 tsp. dry mustard
1 tsp. Worcestershire sauce

2 c. milk
2 c. shredded Cheddar cheese
1½ lb. fully cooked ham, cut into 2″ strips (3 c.)
1 (10-oz.) pkg. frozen peas, thawed

Cut and measure all ingredients before starting to cook.

Pour water into 12″ skillet or electric frypan and heat over high heat (420⁰) 5 minutes or until water boils.

Add potatoes and return to a boil. Reduce heat to low (220⁰). Cover and simmer 20 minutes or until potatoes are tender.

Drain potatoes in colander. Wipe out skillet.

Melt butter in same skillet over medium heat (300⁰), about 2 minutes. Add onion and sauté 2 minutes. Blend in flour, mustard and Worcestershire sauce. Gradually stir in milk. Cook, stirring constantly, until mixture boils and thickens, about 10 minutes.

Stir in cheese, ham, peas and potatoes. Reduce heat to low (220⁰). Cover and simmer 15 minutes or until thoroughly heated.

Makes 6 servings.

133/Ham jambalaya

- *Preparation time: 16 minutes*
- *Cooking time: 43 minutes*

A colorful and tasty ham skillet with lots of mushrooms, onion and green pepper. It's flavored with bacon bits and chicken bouillon.

4 strips bacon, diced
1 tblsp. cooking oil
½ lb. fresh mushrooms, sliced
1 c. chopped green pepper
1 c. chopped onion
1 c. sliced celery (⅛")
1 (16-oz.) can tomatoes, cut up

2 c. water
2 chicken bouillon cubes
1 c. uncooked regular rice
2 c. cubed fully cooked ham (½")
½ tsp. paprika
⅛ tsp. pepper

Cut and measure all ingredients before starting to cook.

Fry bacon in 12" skillet or electric frypan over medium heat (350⁰) until browned, about 6 minutes. Remove bacon from skillet and drain on paper towels.

Add oil to bacon drippings in skillet. Add mushrooms, green pepper, onion and celery. Sauté 10 minutes (do not brown). Cover and cook 5 minutes more or until celery is tender.

Stir tomatoes into skillet. Remove mixture from skillet and place in bowl. Rinse out skillet.

Add water and chicken bouillon cubes to same skillet. Place over high heat (400⁰). Cover and cook until mixture comes to a boil, about 2 minutes.

Stir in rice. Reduce heat to low (220⁰) and simmer 15 minutes or until rice is tender and liquid is absorbed.

Stir in tomato mixture, bacon, ham, paprika and pepper. Heat thoroughly, about 5 minutes.

Makes 6 servings.

134/Ham strips
in tomato sauce

• *Preparation time: 25 minutes*
• *Cooking time: 38 minutes*

That leftover Easter ham will be more interesting if you serve it in a colorful, perfectly seasoned combination like this one.

⅓ c. cooking oil
2 c. chopped green pepper
2 c. chopped celery
1 c. chopped onion
1 clove garlic, minced
2 (15-oz.) cans tomato
   sauce

½ tsp. chili powder
1½ lb. fully cooked ham,
   cut into julienne strips
½ c. tomato juice
Tabasco sauce
Hot cooked rice

Cut and measure all ingredients before starting to cook.

Heat oil in 10″ skillet over medium heat 3 minutes or until hot.

Add green pepper, celery, onion and garlic. Sauté 8 minutes or until tender (do not brown).

Stir in tomato sauce and chili powder. Cook until mixture comes to a boil, about 2 minutes. Reduce heat to low and simmer, uncovered, 20 minutes.

Stir in ham, tomato juice and a few drops of Tabasco sauce. Cover and simmer 5 minutes or until thoroughly heated. Serve with rice.

Makes 6 to 8 servings.

135/Ham with lima beans

• Preparation time: 10 minutes
• Cooking time: 40 minutes

This is really a kind of ham-vegetable stew. It's delicious served with corn bread squares, cabbage salad and ice cream sundaes.

3 tblsp. butter or regular
  margarine
1 c. chopped green pepper
½ c. chopped onion
1 clove garlic, minced
1 (28-oz.) can tomatoes,
  cut up
1 c. water

1 (10-oz.) pkg. frozen
  Fordhook lima beans
1 (10-oz.) pkg. frozen corn
1 lb. fully cooked ham
  steak, cut into 1″ cubes
2 tblsp. flour
¼ c. water

Cut and measure all ingredients before starting to cook.

Melt butter in 12″ skillet or electric frypan over medium heat (350⁰), about 2 minutes.

Add green pepper, onion and garlic. Sauté until tender, about 5 minutes.

Stir in tomatoes, 1 c. water, lima beans, corn and ham. Cook until mixture comes to a boil, about 1 minute.

Reduce heat to low (220⁰). Cover and simmer 30 minutes or until lima beans are tender.

Combine flour and ¼ c. water in jar. Cover and shake until blended. Slowly stir into simmering ham mixture. Cook 2 minutes or until thickened. Serve in bowls.

Makes 6 servings.

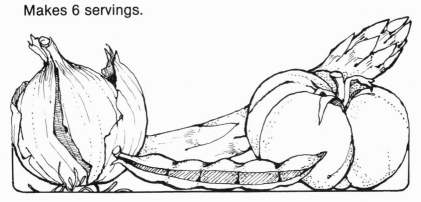

136/Scalloped potatoes with ham

- *Preparation time: 25 minutes*
- *Cooking time: 45 minutes*

You can make scalloped potatoes with fresh green beans and tender chunks of ham without turning on your oven.

5 c. sliced pared potatoes, ¼" thick
1 lb. fresh green beans, cut into 1" pieces
1 c. chopped celery
3 c. water
½ tsp. salt
Milk
¼ c. butter or regular margarine

1 c. chopped onion
¼ c. flour
2 c. cubed fully cooked ham (1")
2 tblsp. chopped fresh parsley
1½ c. shredded Cheddar cheese

Cut and measure all ingredients before starting to cook.

Combine potatoes, green beans, celery, water and salt in 12" skillet or electric frypan. Place over high heat (400⁰) and cook until it comes to a boil, about 5 minutes.

Reduce heat to low (220⁰). Cover and simmer 15 minutes.

Drain vegetables, reserving cooking liquid. Add enough milk to reserved cooking liquid to make 2½ c.; set aside.

Melt butter in same skillet over medium heat (300⁰), about 2 minutes. Add onion and sauté 2 minutes. Remove from heat. Stir in flour. Gradually stir in 2½ c. liquid. Return to medium heat (350⁰). Cook, stirring constantly, until mixture boils and thickens, about 5 minutes. Boil 1 minute.

Stir in drained vegetables, ham and parsley. Turn heat to low (220⁰). Cover and simmer 10 minutes or until thoroughly heated. Sprinkle with Cheddar cheese. Cover and simmer 5 minutes more or until cheese is melted.

Makes 8 servings.

137/Country-style chicken and dumplings

• *Preparation time: 18 minutes*
• *Cooking time: 1 hour 30 minutes*

Few can resist tender pieces of chicken, carrots with peas and fluffy dumplings enveloped in a lightly seasoned chicken gravy.

1 (3-lb.) broiler-fryer, cut up	⅔ c. water
4½ c. water	2 c. thinly sliced onion
¼ c. chopped fresh parsley	1½ c. sliced pared carrots
¾ tsp. poultry seasoning	1 (10-oz.) pkg. frozen peas
4 chicken bouillon cubes	¼ tsp. browning for gravy
¼ tsp. pepper	½ tsp. salt
⅓ c. cornstarch	Dumplings (recipe follows)

Cut and measure all ingredients before starting to cook.

Place chicken, 4½ c. water, parsley, poultry seasoning, chicken bouillon cubes and pepper in 12″ skillet or electric frypan over high heat (400⁰). Cover and cook until it comes to a boil, about 5 minutes. Reduce heat to low (220⁰). Cover and simmer 1 hour or until chicken is tender.

Remove chicken from broth. Cool slightly. Remove meat from bones and cut up. Discard skin and bones. Prepare Dumplings.

Place broth over high heat (400⁰) and bring to a boil, about 3 minutes. Combine cornstarch and ⅔ c. water in bowl; stir to blend. Stir cornstarch mixture into simmering broth. Cook, stirring constantly, until it thickens slightly, about 2 minutes. Add onion, carrots, peas, browning for gravy and salt.

Drop Dumplings by tablespoonfuls into simmering broth. Reduce heat to low (220⁰). Simmer, uncovered, 10 minutes. Cover and simmer 10 minutes more.

Makes 6 servings.

Dumplings: Combine 1½ c. sifted flour, 2 tsp. baking powder and ¾ tsp. salt in bowl. Cut in 3 tblsp. shortening until it looks like coarse meal. Add ¾ c. milk; stir until moistened.

138/Barbecued chicken with peppers

• Preparation time: 6 minutes
• Cooking time: 1 hour

"This barbecued chicken dish is a little different and is so easy to fix. I serve it often," wrote a Kentucky farmer's wife.

¼ c. cooking oil
1 (2½-lb.) broiler-fryer, cut up
1 tsp. salt
¼ c. bottled barbecue sauce
¼ c. water

⅔ c. sliced onion
⅔ c. cut-up green pepper, 1″ squares
1 (3-oz.) can sliced mushrooms, drained
1 tsp. cornstarch
1 tblsp. water

Cut and measure all ingredients before starting to cook.

Heat oil in 12″ skillet or electric frypan over medium-high heat (375⁰), about 5 minutes.

Meanwhile, season chicken with salt.

Brown chicken on all sides in hot oil, turning frequently, 8 minutes.

Add barbecue sauce, ¼ c. water and onion to skillet. Reduce heat to low (220⁰). Cover and simmer 30 minutes.

Add green pepper and mushrooms. Cover and simmer 15 minutes more or until chicken is tender.

Remove chicken from skillet to warm platter. Skim off fat from pan juices.

Combine cornstarch and 1 tblsp. water in small dish; stir to blend. Place skillet over medium heat (350⁰). Slowly stir cornstarch mixture into pan juices. Cook, stirring constantly, until mixture boils and thickens, about 2 minutes. Spoon sauce over chicken.

Makes 4 servings.

139/Creole-style chicken zucchini

- *Preparation time: 18 minutes*
- *Cooking time: 59 minutes*

Chicken is such a good buy today and so versatile. Here's an herb-flavored dish with tomatoes, zucchini and green pepper.

5 tblsp. butter or regular
   margarine
1 (3-lb.) broiler-fryer,
   cut up
1 c. chopped onion
½ c. chopped green pepper
1 clove garlic, minced
⅓ c. flour
1¼ tsp. salt
½ tsp. dried basil leaves
¼ tsp. dried oregano
   leaves
¼ tsp. pepper
1 (13¾-oz.) can chicken
   broth
1 (28-oz.) can Italian
   tomatoes, drained and
   cut up
3 medium zucchini, sliced
2 tblsp. minced fresh
   parsley

Cut and measure all ingredients before starting to cook.

Melt butter in 12″ skillet or electric frypan over medium heat (350⁰), about 2 minutes.

Brown chicken on all sides in melted butter, turning frequently, about 10 minutes. Remove chicken as it browns.

Add onion, green pepper and garlic to pan drippings. Sauté until tender (do not brown), about 5 minutes.

Stir in flour, salt, basil, oregano and pepper. Cook, stirring constantly, 1 minute. Gradually stir in chicken broth and tomatoes. Cook until mixture comes to a boil, about 1 minute. Add chicken. Reduce heat to low (220⁰). Cover and simmer 20 minutes.

Add zucchini; cover and simmer 20 minutes more or until chicken and zucchini are tender. Sprinkle with parsley.

Makes 4 servings.

140/Piquant barbecued chicken

• *Preparation time: 12 minutes*
• *Cooking time: 1 hour 15 minutes*

This recipe is suited to larger families because it cooks two chickens at one time in a zesty barbecue-style sauce.

2 tblsp. cooking oil
½ c. chopped onion
½ c. chopped celery
1 (10¾-oz.) can condensed
   tomato soup
1 c. ketchup
½ c. water
¼ c. lemon juice
3 tblsp. Worcestershire
   sauce

3 tblsp. brown sugar,
   packed
2 tblsp. vinegar
2 tblsp. prepared mustard
2 drops Tabasco sauce
¼ tsp. pepper
2 (3-lb.) broiler-fryers,
   quartered

Cut and measure all ingredients before starting to cook.

Heat oil in 12″ skillet or electric frypan over medium heat (350⁰) 5 minutes or until hot.

Add onion and celery. Sauté 3 minutes or until tender. Stir in tomato soup, ketchup, water, lemon juice, Worcestershire sauce, brown sugar, vinegar, mustard, Tabasco sauce and pepper. Cook until mixture comes to a boil, about 2 minutes.

Reduce heat to low (220⁰). Simmer 15 minutes, stirring occasionally.

Arrange chicken in skillet, spooning sauce over it. Cover and simmer 50 minutes, basting with sauce occasionally.

Makes 8 servings.

141/Chicken 'n' dumplings

• *Preparation time: 10 minutes*
• *Cooking time: 36 minutes*

You'll get perfect dumplings every time when you use this recipe because they're made with buttermilk baking mix.

3 tblsp. butter or regular margarine
½ c. chopped onion
¼ c. chopped green pepper
2 tblsp. flour
2¾ c. tomato juice
1 chicken bouillon cube
½ tsp. salt
¼ tsp. paprika

¼ tsp. dried thyme leaves
⅛ tsp. pepper
2 c. cubed cooked chicken
1 c. frozen peas, thawed
1 c. frozen corn, thawed
2 c. buttermilk baking mix
⅔ c. milk
Minced fresh parsley

Cut and measure all ingredients before starting to cook.

Melt butter in 12″ skillet or electric frypan over medium heat (325⁰), about 2 minutes.

Add onion and green pepper. Sauté until tender (do not brown), about 5 minutes.

Stir in flour and cook 1 minute, stirring constantly. Slowly stir in tomato juice. Add bouillon cube, salt, paprika, thyme and pepper. Cook, stirring constantly, until mixture boils and thickens, about 2 minutes.

Add chicken, peas and corn; mix well. Cook until mixture comes to a boil, about 1 minute. Reduce heat to low (220⁰).

Combine baking mix and milk in bowl. Mix just until blended. Spoon mixture by tablespoonfuls into hot chicken mixture. Cook, uncovered, 10 minutes. Cover and cook 15 minutes more. Sprinkle with parsley.

Makes 6 servings.

142/Basic lamb stew

• *Preparation time: 23 minutes*
• *Cooking time: 1 hour 44 minutes*

A skillet with a tight-fitting lid makes a good stewpot; use it to gently simmer this stew for extra-tender meat and vegetables.

2 lb. boneless lamb, cut into 1″ cubes
1 clove garlic, minced
2 tsp. salt
¼ tsp. pepper
1½ c. water
3 large carrots, pared and cut into lengthwise halves
3 medium potatoes, pared and quartered

1 large onion, coarsely chopped
1 large green pepper, cut into lengthwise strips
¼ c. chopped fresh parsley
2 strips bacon, cut into thirds
1 c. water
Water
4 tsp. cornstarch
2 tblsp. water

Cut and measure all ingredients before starting to cook.

Combine lamb cubes, garlic, salt, pepper and 1½ c. water in 12″ skillet or electric frypan over high heat (400⁰). Cook until mixture comes to a boil, about 7 minutes.

Reduce heat to low (220⁰). Cover and simmer 1 hour.

Add carrots, potatoes, onion, green pepper, parsley, bacon and 1 c. water. Return to a boil, about 2 minutes. Cover and simmer 30 minutes or until lamb and vegetables are tender.

Remove from heat. Drain off pan juices into a measuring cup. Add enough water to make 1 c. Return pan juices to skillet. Combine cornstarch and 2 tblsp. water in bowl; stir until blended. Add cornstarch mixture to stew and place over high heat (400⁰). Cook, stirring constantly, until mixture boils and thickens, about 5 minutes.

Makes 6 servings.

143/Lamb lentil stew

- *Preparation time: 20 minutes*
- *Cooking time: 2 hours 15 minutes*

This is called a stew because it's thicker than most soups. If you prefer to serve it as a soup, just stir in some additional water.

2 tblsp. cooking oil
1 lb. boneless lamb, cut
   into 1" cubes
1 c. chopped onion
1 c. chopped celery
2 cloves garlic, minced
1 (16-oz.) can tomatoes,
   cut up
1 c. water
2 tsp. chicken bouillon
   granules

1 tsp. salt
½ tsp. dried oregano
   leaves
¼ tsp. pepper
1 bay leaf
1 c. dried lentils
2 c. sliced pared carrots
2½ c. water

Cut and measure all ingredients before starting to cook.

Heat oil in 12" skillet or electric frypan over medium heat (350°) 5 minutes or until hot.

Brown lamb cubes in hot oil, about 10 minutes. Pour off excess fat from skillet.

Add onion, celery, garlic, tomatoes, 1 c. water, chicken bouillon granules, salt, oregano, pepper and bay leaf. Reduce heat to low (220°). Cover and simmer 1 hour.

Rinse lentils. Add lentils, carrots and 2½ c. water. Cover and simmer 1 hour, stirring occasionally. (Add water if necessary.)

Makes 6 servings.

144/Spaghetti with haddock

- *Preparation time: 21 minutes*
- *Cooking time: 35 minutes*

Here's an easy way to prepare the inexpensive frozen 1-lb. blocks of fish. Just thaw and cut into squares instead of separating the fillets.

2 (1-lb.) pkg. frozen
haddock fillets, thawed
3 tblsp. cooking oil
½ lb. fresh mushrooms,
sliced
1 clove garlic, minced
2 (10¾-oz.) cans
condensed cream of
mushroom soup
1¼ c. milk

1¼ c. grated Parmesan
cheese
8 oz. spaghetti, cooked
and drained
2 tblsp. chopped fresh
parsley
1 (10-oz.) pkg. frozen
chopped spinach,
thawed and drained

Cut and measure all ingredients before starting to cook.

Do not separate haddock fillets. Cut each block of haddock into 3 pieces; set aside.

Heat oil in 12″ skillet or electric frypan over medium heat (300⁰) 5 minutes or until hot.

Add mushrooms and garlic. Sauté 10 minutes or until tender. Remove from skillet.

Combine mushroom soup, milk and 1 c. of the Parmesan cheese in skillet. Stir until blended. Add spaghetti and parsley. Toss until coated. Arrange fish on top.

Combine mushrooms and spinach. Arrange on top of fish. Cover and cook over low heat (220⁰) 10 minutes.

Sprinkle with remaining ¼ c. Parmesan cheese. Cover and simmer 10 minutes more or until fish flakes with fork.

Makes 6 servings.

145/Landlubber's seafood chowder

- *Preparation time: 16 minutes*
- *Cooking time: 1 hour 1 minute*

You don't have to live near the sea to enjoy fish chowder, because you can use canned minced clams and frozen haddock fillets.

3 tblsp. butter or regular margarine
1 c. chopped onion
1 c. sliced celery, ⅛" thick
¼ c. chopped fresh parsley
½ tsp. dried rosemary leaves
2 c. cubed pared potatoes (½")
1 c. sliced pared carrots, ⅛" thick

1 (16-oz.) can stewed tomatoes
2 c. chicken broth
1 tsp. salt
3 tblsp. flour
2 (6½-oz.) cans chopped clams
1 (1-lb.) pkg. frozen haddock, thawed and cut into 1" pieces
1 c. light cream

Cut and measure all ingredients before starting to cook.

Melt butter in 12" skillet or electric frypan over medium heat (350⁰) 4 minutes.

Add onion, celery, parsley and rosemary; sauté 7 minutes. Stir in potatoes, carrots, tomatoes, 1½ c. of the chicken broth and salt. Bring mixture to a boil over medium-high heat (375⁰), about 3 minutes.

Reduce heat to low (220⁰). Cover and simmer 30 minutes.

Increase heat to medium (350⁰). Combine flour and remaining chicken broth in jar. Cover and shake until blended. Stir into simmering soup. Cook, stirring constantly, until mixture comes to a boil, about 2 minutes.

Add clams with juice and haddock. Cook until mixture comes to a boil, about 5 minutes. Reduce heat to low (220⁰). Simmer 8 minutes or until fish flakes easily with fork.

Stir in light cream and heat 2 minutes more.

Makes 8 servings.

146/Tuna burgers with noodles

• Preparation time: 15 minutes
• Cooking time: 34 minutes

This dinner is the brainchild of one of our home economists: Lightly seasoned tuna burgers nestled in a bed of creamy noodles.

2 c. water
½ tsp. salt
1 (10-oz.) pkg. frozen cut green beans
2 (7-oz.) cans chunk-style tuna, drained and flaked
¾ c. soft bread crumbs
½ c. finely chopped celery
¼ c. minced onion
2 tblsp. chopped fresh parsley
1 egg

⅔ c. mayonnaise
¼ tsp. pepper
2 tblsp. butter or regular margarine
1 (10¾-oz.) can condensed cream of chicken soup
¾ c. milk
1½ c. dairy sour cream
8 oz. wide noodles, cooked and drained
1½ tsp. dried dillweed

Cut and assemble all ingredients before starting to cook.

Combine water and salt in 12″ skillet or electric frypan over high heat (400⁰). Cook until mixture comes to a boil, about 3 minutes. Add beans and return to a boil. Reduce heat to low (220⁰). Cover and simmer 10 minutes or until tender. Drain beans in colander. Wipe out skillet.

Meanwhile, combine tuna, bread crumbs, celery, onion, parsley, egg, mayonnaise and pepper in bowl. Mix lightly, but well. Shape mixture into 6 patties.

Melt butter in same skillet over medium heat (300⁰), about 2 minutes. Brown patties on both sides in butter, about 4 minutes. Remove patties from skillet.

Combine chicken soup and milk in skillet; mix until blended. Stir in sour cream. Add noodles, dillweed and cooked beans. Stir until well mixed. Place burgers on top.

Reduce heat to low (220⁰). Cover and simmer 15 minutes. Makes 6 servings.

147/Quick salmon chowder

- *Preparation time: 10 minutes*
- *Cooking time: 36 minutes*

This recipe was originally developed to take on a camping trip, but it's good for a fast, nourishing meal any time.

6 strips bacon, diced
½ c. chopped onion
1 (10¾-oz.) can condensed chicken broth
1 (5½-oz.) pkg. au gratin potato mix
2 c. water
1½ c. milk

1 (17-oz.) can whole-kernel corn
⅛ tsp. pepper
1 (15½-oz.) can red sockeye salmon, drained, skinned, boned and broken into chunks
⅓ c. evaporated milk

Cut and measure all ingredients before starting to cook.

Fry bacon in 12″ skillet or electric frypan over medium heat (350⁰) until browned, about 8 minutes. Remove bacon with slotted spoon and drain on paper towels.

Drain off all but 2 tblsp. bacon drippings. Sauté onion in bacon drippings over medium heat (350⁰) 4 minutes or until tender.

Stir in bacon, chicken broth, au gratin potato mix (including sauce mix), water, milk, corn, and pepper. Cook over high heat (400⁰) until mixture comes to a boil, about 4 minutes.

Reduce heat to low (220⁰). Cover and simmer 15 minutes.

Stir in salmon and evaporated milk. Cover and simmer 5 minutes or until thoroughly heated.

Makes 2 quarts.

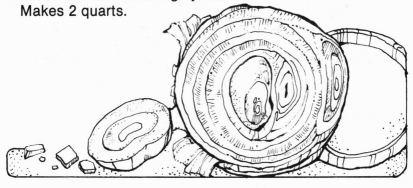

148/Wagon-wheel sausage supper

- *Preparation time: 18 minutes*
- *Cooking time: 17 minutes*

You can enjoy hash browns without spending a lot of time paring and shredding potatoes. The potato mix sure is a timesaver!

1 (6-oz.) pkg. hash brown
  potato mix
4 c. very hot water
1½ tsp. salt
⅓ c. chopped onion
⅓ c. chopped green pepper

1 (8-oz.) pkg. brown and
  serve link pork sausage
2 tblsp. butter or regular
  margarine
2 c. shredded Cheddar
  cheese

Combine hash brown potato mix, very hot water and salt in bowl; mix to blend. Let stand 15 minutes.

Meanwhile, cut and measure remaining ingredients.

Drain potato mixture. Add onion and green pepper; mix well. Set mixture aside.

Cook link pork sausage in 10″ skillet over medium heat 8 minutes or until browned, turning sausage frequently. Remove sausage from skillet and drain on paper towels.

Add butter to skillet and place over medium-high heat. 1 minute or until melted. Evenly spread drained potato mixture in skillet. Cook, without stirring, 5 minutes or until well browned on bottom.

Turn potato mixture over carefully with spatula. Sprinkle with Cheddar cheese. Arrange sausage links on top like spokes of a wheel. Cover and cook 3 minutes more.

Cut into wedges.

Makes 5 servings.

149/Mexicali tamale skillet

- *Preparation time: 20 minutes*
- *Cooking time: 33 minutes*

A mildly spicy sausage, tomato and lima bean skillet flavored with chili powder and topped with a tender layer of corn bread.

1½ lb. bulk pork sausage
1 c. chopped onion
¾ c. chopped green pepper
1 clove garlic, minced
¾ c. sifted flour
¾ c. yellow corn meal
1 tsp. baking powder
1 tsp. salt
½ tsp. baking soda
1 c. sour milk
1 egg, beaten
2 tblsp. cooking oil

1 (16-oz.) can stewed tomatoes
2 (8-oz.) cans tomato sauce
2 (10-oz.) pkg. frozen Fordhook lima beans, thawed
¼ tsp. salt
⅛ tsp. pepper
2 tblsp. chili powder
1 c. shredded Cheddar cheese

Cut and measure all ingredients before starting to cook.

Cook sausage, onion, green pepper and garlic in 12″ skillet or electric frypan over high heat (400⁰) 10 minutes or until well browned. Drain off excess fat.

Meanwhile, sift together flour, corn meal, baking powder, 1 tsp. salt and baking soda into bowl. Add sour milk, egg and oil. Stir just until moistened and set aside.

Add tomatoes, tomato sauce, lima beans, ¼ tsp. salt, pepper, chili powder and cheese to skillet. Cook until mixture comes to a boil, about 1 minute. Simmer 4 minutes.

Spread corn meal mixture evenly over all. Reduce heat to low (220⁰). Cover and simmer 18 minutes or until topping tests done.

Remove from heat. Uncover and let stand 5 minutes before serving.

Makes 6 to 8 servings.

150/Upside-down sausage 'n' stuffing

- *Preparation time: 10 minutes*
- *Cooking time: 35 minutes*

Sausage, stuffing and peas with carrots make an interesting meal that's inverted onto a plate and cut into wedges before serving.

1 lb. bulk pork sausage
½ c. soft bread crumbs
½ c. chopped onion
1 (10½-oz.) can chicken gravy
1 tblsp. chopped fresh parsley
¼ tsp. rubbed sage
1 egg, beaten
1 (10-oz.) pkg. frozen peas and carrots

¼ c. water
1 (6-oz.) pkg. instant stuffing mix, chicken flavor
1½ c. very hot water
¼ c. melted butter or regular margarine
1 egg, beaten

Cut and measure all ingredients before starting to cook.

Combine sausage, bread crumbs, onion, ⅓ c. of the chicken gravy, parsley, sage and 1 egg in bowl. Mix well. Pat sausage mixture into 10″ skillet forming a 2¼″ wide ring.

Place over medium-low heat and cover. Cook 15 minutes.

Drain off excess fat from skillet. Place peas and carrots with ¼ c. water in center of ring. Combine stuffing mix, 1½ c. very hot water, butter and seasoning packet from stuffing mix in bowl. Stir until moistened. Stir in 1 egg.

Evenly spread stuffing mixture over sausage and vegetables in skillet. Cover and cook 18 minutes.

Remove skillet from heat. Uncover and let stand 5 minutes.

Meanwhile, reheat remaining gravy in small saucepan over medium heat, about 2 minutes.

Loosen edges with spatula. Invert skillet over serving plate and remove. Serve with warm gravy.

Makes 6 servings.

151/Zucchini with sausage and cheese

• Preparation time: 20 minutes
• Cooking time: 1 hour 7 minutes

Zucchini, sausage sauce, cottage cheese and mozzarella cheese are layered carefully into a skillet before simmering.

1½ c. water
2 lb. zucchini, sliced
½ lb. bulk pork sausage
½ c. chopped onion
1 clove garlic, minced
1 (16-oz.) can tomatoes, puréed in blender
1 (6-oz.) can tomato paste
1 (4-oz.) can mushrooms, drained
2 tsp. dried oregano leaves

1 tsp. dried basil leaves
1 (16-oz.) carton creamed small-curd cottage cheese
½ c. grated Parmesan cheese
2 tblsp. chopped fresh parsley
⅓ c. fine dry bread crumbs
2 c. shredded mozzarella cheese

Cut and measure all ingredients before starting to cook.

Combine water and zucchini in 10″ skillet over high heat and cook until it comes to a boil, about 4 minutes. Cover and cook 5 minutes or until zucchini is tender-crisp. Drain well.

Cook sausage, onion and garlic in same skillet over medium heat 10 minutes or until browned. Stir in tomatoes, tomato paste, mushrooms, oregano and basil. Cook until mixture comes to a boil, about 1 minute. Reduce heat to low. Cover and simmer 15 minutes.

Pour sauce into a bowl and rinse out skillet. Combine cottage cheese, Parmesan cheese and parsley; set aside.

Spoon 1 c. of the sauce into same skillet. Top with one-half of zucchini and then one-half of bread crumbs. Then, layer in one-half of cottage cheese mixture and top with one-half of sauce. Repeat layers starting with zucchini. Place over low heat. Cover and simmer 30 minutes. Sprinkle with mozzarella cheese. Cover; simmer 2 minutes or until cheese melts.

Makes 4 to 6 servings.

152/Mexican-style macaroni supper

- *Preparation time: 10 minutes*
- *Cooking time: 48 minutes*

"I like this because it can be prepared in a short time and my family likes it because it's Mexican," said a North Dakota woman.

1 lb. bulk pork sausage	2 tblsp. sugar
¾ c. chopped onion	1 tblsp. chili powder
¾ c. chopped green pepper	1 tsp. salt
1 (28-oz.) can tomatoes, cut up	2 c. uncooked elbow macaroni
1 pt. dairy sour cream	Minced fresh parsley
¾ c. water	

Cut and measure all ingredients before starting to cook.

Cook sausage, onion and green pepper in 12″ skillet or electric frypan over medium heat (350⁰) 10 minutes or until well browned.

Meanwhile, combine tomatoes, sour cream, water, sugar, chili powder and salt in bowl; stir to blend.

Pour off excess fat from skillet. Stir tomato mixture into sausage mixture, mixing well with spoon. Add uncooked elbow macaroni. Cook until mixture comes to a boil, about 3 minutes.

Reduce heat to low (220⁰). Cover and simmer 35 minutes or until macaroni is tender, stirring occasionally. Sprinkle with parsley.

Makes 6 to 8 servings.

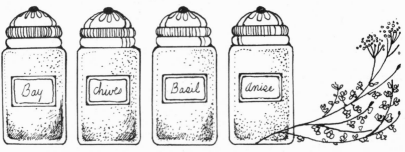

Plate 5: Terrific for lunch and casual get-togethers, versatile Beef Barbecue Buns (p. 94) are heaped high with thinly sliced beef in a spicy barbecue sauce.

Plate 6: This super-crisp
Pepperoni Cheese Pizza
(p. 34) bakes in an electric
frypan in only 17 minutes
and uses less energy than
when baked in an oven.

Plate 7: Cheesy Egg Puff
(p. 47) is an omelet-quiche
topped with an oregano-
spiked tomato sauce and
blanketed with melted
Cheddar cheese and crisp
bacon bits.

Plate 8: Protein-packed
Noodle Frank Skillet (p. 42)
is a timesaver and a budget-
stretcher. It features cottage
cheese-sauced noodles.

153/Italian-style crepes

- *Preparation time: 10 minutes*
- *Cooking time: 54 minutes*

These unusual crepes are wrapped around a pizza-flavored pepperoni mixture and melted provolone cheese.

Crepes (recipe follows)
5 tblsp. cooking oil
½ lb. fresh mushrooms, sliced
½ c. chopped onion
1 clove garlic, minced
½ lb. sliced pepperoni

1 (6-oz.) can tomato paste
1 tsp. dried oregano leaves
6 oz. sliced provolone cheese
6 tblsp. grated Romano cheese

Cut and measure all ingredients before starting to cook.

Prepare Crepes. Heat 10″ skillet over medium-high heat 1 minute. Brush skillet with ½ tsp. of the oil. Pour a scant ⅓ c. crepe batter into skillet, tilting to coat entire bottom surface of skillet. Bake 2 minutes or until lightly browned. Loosen edges of crepe with metal spatula. Turn over and bake 2 minutes more or until lightly browned. Remove and place on waxed paper. Repeat with remaining batter, using ½ tsp. of the oil for each, about 20 minutes. Makes a total of 6 crepes. Stack crepes between waxed paper.

Heat 3 tblsp. of the oil in skillet over medium heat 1 minute. Add mushrooms, onion and garlic. Sauté 7 minutes. Remove from heat. Stir in pepperoni, tomato paste and oregano. Place ⅓ c. pepperoni mixture in center of each crepe. Top with ⅙ of the provolone and 1 tblsp. of the Romano cheese.

Fold two sides of crepe over filling, about 1″. Then fold opposite side and then overlap remaining side (like envelope).

Heat remaining 1 tblsp. oil in skillet, about 1 minute. Carefully arrange crepes in skillet, seam side down. Cook 10 minutes and turn over. Cook 10 minutes or until crispy.

Makes 6 crepes.

Crepes: Combine ¾ c. sifted flour, ¼ tsp. salt, 2 eggs and 1 c. milk in bowl. Beat until smooth.

FAMILY-STYLE FAVORITES

154/Country skillet supper

• Preparation time: 2 minutes
• Cooking time: 1 hour

"When I want to make this recipe, I cook extra potatoes the day before," wrote the Washington woman who shared it with us.

6 c. water	8 strips bacon, diced
1½ lb. kielbasa or smoked pork sausage	4 medium onions
3 lb. potatoes, cooked and drained	2 large green peppers
	½ tsp. salt
	⅛ tsp. pepper

Cut and measure all ingredients before starting to cook.

Heat 6 c. water in 12″ skillet or electric frypan over high heat (400⁰) 5 minutes or until it comes to a boil.

Add kielbasa. Reduce heat to low (220⁰). Simmer, uncovered, 15 minutes.

Meanwhile, peel potatoes. Cut into 1″ cubes; set aside. Remove kielbasa from skillet; set aside. Pour off water from skillet and wipe out with paper towels.

Cook bacon in same skillet over medium heat (325⁰) 10 minutes or until browned. Meanwhile, chop onion and cut green peppers into 1″ squares and set aside.

Remove bacon from skillet and drain on paper towels. Add onion and green pepper to bacon drippings and sauté 5 minutes. Add potatoes, salt and pepper, and sauté until lightly browned, about 15 minutes.

Meanwhile, cut kielbasa into ½″ slices. Add kielbasa to skillet. Reduce heat to low (200⁰). Cook 10 minutes.

Sprinkle with bacon before serving.

Makes 6 to 8 servings.

155/Quick-cook vegetable scallop

- *Preparation time: 20 minutes*
- *Cooking time: 37 minutes*

"This is a quickie meal perfect for the farm. I hope others will like it, too," wrote a Kansas woman across the bottom of the recipe.

1 (10¾-oz.) can condensed cream of mushroom soup
1 c. water
2 lb. unpared potatoes, thinly sliced
½ tsp. salt
⅛ tsp. pepper
1 (12-oz.) can pork luncheon meat, cut into 2 × ½" sticks

1 c. sliced onion, separated into rings
¼ c. thinly sliced celery
2 large tomatoes, sliced
2 c. shredded Cheddar cheese

Cut and measure all ingredients before starting to cook.

Combine mushroom soup and water in bowl; mix until blended. Spoon 1 c. of the soup mixture into 12" skillet or electric frypan.

Arrange potatoes on top of soup. Sprinkle potatoes with salt and pepper. Then layer in remaining ingredients, starting with pork luncheon meat, onion rings, celery and tomatoes.

Pour remaining soup mixture over all. Cover and cook over medium heat (350°) 4 minutes or until mixture comes to a boil.

Reduce heat to low (220°). Cover and simmer 30 minutes more.

Sprinkle with cheese. Cover and cook 3 minutes more or until cheese is melted.

Makes 4 to 6 servings.

156/Corn meal pancakes with franks

- Preparation time: 12 minutes
- Cooking time: 31 minutes

A supper dish that children are sure to like. Light and delicate corn meal pancakes topped with a spicy sauce made with frankfurters.

1 (12-oz.) pkg. corn muffin mix
1 egg
1¾ c. milk
1 tblsp. cooking oil
1 lb. frankfurters
2 tblsp. butter or regular margarine
2 (10¾-oz.) cans condensed tomato soup

2 tblsp. finely chopped onion
2 tblsp. brown sugar, packed
1 tblsp. cider vinegar
1 tsp. Worcestershire sauce

Cut and measure all ingredients before starting to cook.

Combine corn muffin mix, egg and milk in bowl. Stir just until moistened.

Heat oil in 12″ skillet or electric frypan over medium heat (350⁰) 5 minutes or until hot.

Pour batter into skillet, using scant ¼ c. for each pancake.

Bake until evenly browned, about 1½ minutes. Turn over and bake 1½ minutes more. Remove and keep warm. Repeat with remaining batter, about 12 minutes more.

Cut frankfurters into eight thin strips and then cut each strip in half. Melt butter in same skillet over medium heat (300⁰), about 2 minutes.

Add frankfurters and cook until lightly browned, about 4 minutes. Stir in tomato soup, onion, brown sugar, vinegar and Worcestershire sauce. Reduce heat to low (220⁰). Simmer, uncovered, until thoroughly heated, about 5 minutes.

Use 3 to 4 pancakes for each serving. Spoon frankfurter filling over stack of pancakes.

Makes 5 to 6 servings.

157/Tomato and bacon pizza with homemade crust

- *Preparation time: 39 minutes*
- *Cooking time: 34 minutes*

This pizza has an interesting topping made of sliced Swiss cheese, bacon bits and a basil-scented tomato sauce. Very unusual!

1 pkg. dry active yeast	½ lb. bacon, diced
½ c. lukewarm water (110°)	2 tsp. cornstarch
1 tblsp. cooking oil	½ tsp. dried basil leaves
1 tsp. sugar	⅛ tsp. pepper
¾ tsp. salt	¼ c. chopped onion
1½ c. sifted flour	6 oz. sliced Swiss cheese
1 (14½-oz.) can Italian tomatoes	⅓ c. grated Romano cheese

Measure ingredients for pizza crust. Dissolve yeast in luke-warm water in bowl; mix well. Stir in oil, sugar, salt and ¾ c. of the flour. Stir in enough remaining flour to make a soft dough.

Turn dough out onto floured surface and knead until smooth, about 5 minutes. Place in greased bowl, turning once to grease top. Cover and let rise in warm place until doubled, about 30 minutes. Cut and measure remaining ingredients. Drain tomatoes, reserving juice. Slice tomatoes.

Fry bacon in 12″ electric frypan over medium heat (350°) 6 minutes or until browned. Remove and drain on paper towels. Drain fat from skillet. Turn heat to low (220°).

Stir cornstarch, basil, pepper and reserved tomato juice into frypan. Stir in tomatoes. Cook, stirring constantly, until mixture boils and thickens, about 3 minutes. Pour into a bowl.

Grease same frypan with shortening. Pat pizza dough into bottom and ¾″ up sides. Spread tomato mixture over dough. Sprinkle with onion. Cover with Swiss cheese; sprinkle with bacon and Romano cheese.

Set heat to medium (300°). Cover and bake 25 minutes or until crust is browned and crispy. Cut into squares.

Makes 8 servings.

FAMILY-STYLE FAVORITES

158/Bacon noodle skillet

• *Preparation time: 12 minutes*
• *Cooking time: 52 minutes*

The noodles cook right along with the rest of the ingredients in this flavorful dish of bacon, green pepper, onion and stewed tomatoes.

1 lb. bacon
½ c. chopped green pepper
½ c. chopped onion
1 tsp. salt
½ tsp. dried marjoram leaves
½ tsp. dried thyme leaves
⅛ tsp. pepper

2 (16-oz.) cans stewed tomatoes
2 c. water
8 oz. uncooked wide noodles
1½ c. shredded Cheddar cheese

Cut and measure all ingredients before starting to cook.

Fry bacon in 10″ skillet until crisp, removing bacon as it browns. (Total cooking time: 20 minutes.) Drain bacon on paper towels.

Pour off all but 2 tblsp. bacon drippings. Add green pepper and onion to bacon drippings. Sauté over medium heat 5 minutes or until tender.

Stir in salt, marjoram, thyme, pepper, stewed tomatoes and water. Cook until mixture comes to a boil, about 2 minutes.

Add noodles. Reduce heat to low. Cover and simmer 20 minutes.

Crumble half of the bacon. Stir crumbled bacon into skillet. Sprinkle with cheese and garnish with remaining bacon strips.

Cover and simmer 5 minutes or until cheese melts.

Makes 6 servings.

159/Country breakfast skillet

- *Preparation time: 15 minutes*
- *Cooking time: 52 minutes*

Eggs, ham and potatoes are combined in one skillet and topped with melted Cheddar cheese. Sure saves on cleanup time!

3 c. water	2½ c. cubed fully cooked
1 tsp. salt	ham (½″)
4 c. sliced pared potatoes	6 eggs
4 tblsp. butter or regular	½ tsp. salt
margarine	⅛ tsp. pepper
1 c. chopped onion	2 c. shredded Cheddar
1 c. chopped green pepper	cheese

Cut and measure all ingredients before starting to cook.

Heat water and 1 tsp. salt in 12″ skillet or electric frypan over high heat (400⁰) 4 minutes or until it comes to a boil. Add potatoes and return to a boil, about 2 minutes.

Reduce heat to low (220⁰). Cover and cook 5 minutes. Drain in colander. Melt 2 tblsp. of the butter in skillet over medium heat (350⁰), about 2 minutes. Add onion and green pepper; sauté 4 minutes. Remove sautéed vegetables; set aside.

Add remaining 2 tblsp. butter. Place over medium heat (350⁰) until melted, about 2 minutes. Remove from heat.

Place one half of the potatoes in bottom of skillet and top with one half of the sautéed vegetables. Repeat layers. Top with ham cubes. Cover and cook over low heat (220⁰) 20 minutes or until potatoes are tender.

Combine eggs, ½ tsp. salt and pepper in bowl. Beat with rotary beater until blended. Pour over ham mixture. Cover and cook 10 minutes more or until eggs are set.

Sprinkle with cheese. Cover and cook 3 minutes more or until cheese is melted.

Makes 8 servings.

160/Bacon potato puff

• *Preparation time: 20 minutes*
• *Cooking time: 33 minutes*

Not really an omelet, but more like a puffy mashed potato pancake filled with bacon and cheese. Good for either breakfast or brunch.

8 strips bacon
6 eggs, separated
1½ tsp. baking powder
¼ tsp. salt
⅛ tsp. pepper
3 tblsp. milk

1½ c. prepared instant mashed potatoes
4 slices process American cheese, cut into ¼" strips

Cut and measure all ingredients before starting to cook.

Fry bacon in 12″ skillet or electric frypan over medium heat (350⁰) 6 minutes or until browned. Remove from skillet and drain on paper towels. Crumble bacon and set aside.

Beat egg yolks in bowl until thick and lemon-colored, using electric mixer at high speed. Blend in baking powder, salt, pepper and milk; beat well. Stir in potatoes and set aside.

Beat egg whites in another bowl until stiff, but not dry, peaks form, using electric mixer at high speed. Gently fold egg yolk mixture into egg whites.

Pour off all but 2 tblsp. bacon drippings from skillet. Heat skillet over medium-low heat (250⁰) 2 minutes.

Pour in egg mixture, spreading evenly. Cook 10 minutes.

Cover and cook 15 minutes more or until bottom is golden brown and center is set.

Loosen edges. Slide onto heated platter. Sprinkle with bacon and cheese strips. Fold in half.

Makes 4 to 6 servings.

161/Eggs and vegetables Provencale

• *Preparation time: 30 minutes*
• *Cooking time: 39 minutes*

Mushrooms, onion, zucchini and tomatoes combined with softly cooked eggs make an excellent end-of-summer supper.

3 tblsp. cooking oil
1 lb. fresh mushrooms,
sliced
1 c. chopped onion
1½ lb. zucchini, sliced
4 large tomatoes, coarsely
chopped (2 lbs.)

1 (8-oz.) can tomato sauce
1 tsp. salt
⅛ tsp. pepper
6 eggs

Cut and measure all ingredients before starting to cook.

Heat oil in 12″ skillet or electric frypan over medium heat (350⁰) 5 minutes or until hot.

Add mushrooms and onion. Sauté until tender (do not brown), about 5 minutes.

Add zucchini, tomatoes, tomato sauce, salt and pepper. Mix well. Cook until mixture comes to a boil, about 2 minutes.

Reduce heat to low (220⁰). Simmer, uncovered, 25 minutes or until vegetables are tender and mixture is thickened.

Make 6 depressions in hot vegetable mixture, using the back of a spoon. Break eggs into depressions. Cover and cook 2 minutes or until whites are set.

Makes 6 servings.

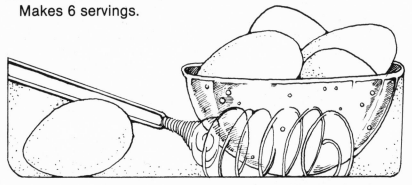

162/Parmesan zucchini and tomatoes

• Preparation time: 32 minutes
• Cooking time: 1 hour 30 minutes

An Iowa farm woman told us that her family likes zucchini when it's cooked this way. The recipe was originally her sister's.

½ c. cooking oil
2 c. chopped green pepper
1½ c. chopped onion
2 cloves garlic, minced
6 c. sliced zucchini (2 lb.)
8 medium tomatoes,
   peeled and chopped

1 tblsp. salt
½ tsp. pepper
2 tsp. cornstarch
2 tblsp. water
½ c. grated Parmesan
   cheese

Cut and measure all ingredients before starting to cook.

Heat oil in 12″ skillet or electric frypan over medium heat (350⁰) 5 minutes or until hot.

Add green pepper, onion and garlic. Sauté 10 minutes or until vegetables are tender (do not brown).

Add zucchini, tomatoes, salt and pepper to skillet. Cook until mixture comes to a boil, about 3 minutes. Reduce heat to low (220⁰). Cover and simmer 15 minutes, stirring occasionally.

Uncover and continue cooking 55 minutes more or until mixture is thickened.

Combine cornstarch and water in bowl; stir to blend. Stir into zucchini mixture. Cook over medium heat (350⁰), stirring constantly, until mixture boils and thickens, about 2 minutes. Sprinkle with Parmesan cheese before serving.

Makes 6 to 8 servings.

163/Viennese potato salad

• *Preparation time: 25 minutes*
• *Cooking time: 31 minutes*

The small sausages make this German-style potato salad a meal in itself. It's served warm with a sprinkle of chopped fresh parsley.

3 lb. salad potatoes,
    cooked and drained
½ lb. bacon, diced
3 tblsp. flour
3 tblsp. brown sugar,
    packed
1 tsp. salt
1½ tsp. dry mustard
1 tsp. celery seeds

⅛ tsp. pepper
1½ c. water
⅔ c. cider vinegar
1 c. chopped onion
3 hard-cooked eggs,
    chopped
4 (5-oz.) cans Vienna
    sausage, drained
Chopped fresh parsley

Cut and measure all ingredients before starting to cook.

When potatoes are cool enough to handle, remove skins. Cut into thin slices and place in bowl.

Fry bacon in 12″ skillet or electric frypan over medium heat (350⁰) until browned, about 6 minutes. Remove bacon with slotted spoon and drain on paper towels.

Pour off all but ⅓ c. bacon drippings from skillet and reduce heat to medium (325⁰). Stir in flour, brown sugar, salt, dry mustard, celery seeds and pepper. Slowly stir in water and vinegar. Cook, stirring constantly, until mixture comes to a boil, about 10 minutes.

Stir in sliced potatoes, onion, eggs and sausage. Reduce heat to low (220⁰). Cover and heat thoroughly 15 minutes, stirring occasionally. Sprinkle with parsley.

Makes 6 to 8 servings.

164/Old-fashioned potato salad

- *Preparation time: 1 hour 20 minutes*
- *Cooking time: 12 minutes*

We cooked the potatoes separately in a Dutch oven, but they can be cooked in the skillet before you begin the other steps.

2 lb. salad potatoes, cooked and drained
⅓ c. cooking oil
¼ c. cider vinegar
1 tblsp. sugar
¾ tsp. garlic salt
½ tsp. salt
⅛ tsp. pepper
¼ tsp. celery seeds

6 strips bacon, diced
¾ c. finely chopped onion
1 tblsp. flour
1 c. water
2 tblsp. chopped green pepper
1 tblsp. minced fresh parsley

Cut and measure all ingredients before starting to cook.

When potatoes are cool enough to handle, remove skins. Cut into ¼" slices and place in bowl.

Combine oil, vinegar, sugar, garlic salt, salt, pepper and celery seeds in another bowl; mix to blend. Pour over potatoes and let stand 1 hour at room temperature to marinate.

Fry bacon in 10" skillet over medium heat until browned, about 6 minutes. Remove bacon with slotted spoon and drain on paper towels.

Pour off all but 2 tblsp. bacon drippings from skillet. Add ½ c. of the onion and sauté over medium heat until tender, about 3 minutes. Stir in flour. Gradually add water, stirring constantly, until mixture boils and thickens, about 2 minutes.

Add potato mixture, remaining ¼ c. onion, green pepper and parsley to skillet. Heat 1 minute. Serve topped with bacon bits.

Makes 4 to 6 servings.

4 Company-pleasing specialties

Country entertaining is traditionally relaxed and informal, so we chose recipes for this section that look especially attractive and appeal to a wide range of palates.

Each recipe in this chapter has something special to offer, yet is easy to prepare, such as our jumbo pasta shells stuffed with a ricotta cheese mixture and sprinkled with Romano cheese. One Minnesota farm woman told us that she serves this dish often because "it takes only ten minutes to prepare, so I can have it ready in no time for unexpected dinner guests."

There are recipes for meat-and-potato fanciers, too: Steak with Sour Cream Gravy, Summer Chicken with Peas, and Pork Steaks with Mushroom Gravy. Each one makes a generous amount of velvety gravy to ladle over potatoes.

Since a meal at any time of day can be a company meal, we've included a variety of main dishes. A perfect choice for brunch is Asparagus Crepes. For a quick luncheon, plan a menu around Ham and Cauliflower Chowder—just add a crisp green salad tossed with an oil and vinegar dressing and a fresh fruit cup for dessert. Our dinner selections include Classic Stroganoff, Veal Parmesan, Sweet-sour Spareribs and Spanish Shrimp with Rice.

Each recipe in this chapter is designed to help you stay out of the kitchen and in the company of your friends so that you can enjoy the party, too.

166/Elegant beef fillets

- *Preparation time: 7 minutes*
- *Cooking time: 30 minutes*

"I have made this recipe many times for friends," a Maryland farm woman wrote to us, "and it's always a hit."

1 tblsp. cooking oil	¼ c. dry red wine
1 tblsp. butter or regular margarine	¼ c. water
4 (8-oz.) beef fillets, 1″ thick	1 tblsp. lemon juice
½ lb. fresh mushrooms, sliced	2 tsp. ketchup
2 tblsp. finely chopped onion	½ tsp. salt
	⅛ tsp. pepper
	1 tblsp. chopped fresh parsley

Cut and measure all ingredients before starting to cook.

Heat oil and butter in 12″ skillet or electric frypan over medium heat (350º) 5 minutes or until hot.

Add beef fillets and cook 5 minutes. Turn over and cook on other side 5 minutes. (This cooking time is for rare. If you would like a more well done steak, cook longer.)

Remove beef fillets to warm platter.

Add mushrooms and onion to pan drippings. Sauté over medium heat (350º) 10 minutes or until tender.

Stir in wine, water, lemon juice, ketchup, salt and pepper. Cook until mixture comes to a boil and boil until volume is reduced to half, about 5 minutes.

Pour sauce over beef and garnish with parsley.

Makes 4 servings.

167/Classic stroganoff

• *Preparation time: 18 minutes*
• *Cooking time: 23 minutes*

An elegant meal for those extra-special dinner guests; as a bonus for the cook, it's not very time-consuming to prepare.

6 tblsp. butter or regular margarine
1½ lb. beef sirloin steak, cut into 2 × ¼″ strips
¾ lb. fresh mushrooms, sliced
1 c. thinly sliced onion
2 cloves garlic, minced
1 tsp. paprika
½ tsp. salt
⅛ tsp. pepper

3 tsp. beef bouillon granules
2 tblsp. ketchup
2 tsp. Worcestershire sauce
4 tblsp. flour
1⅓ c. water
1 c. dairy sour cream
8 oz. noodles, cooked and drained
Chopped fresh parsley

Cut and measure all ingredients before starting to cook.

Melt 2 tblsp. of the butter in 12″ skillet or electric frypan over high heat (375⁰), about 2 minutes.

Add beef strips and cook 5 minutes or until well browned. Remove from skillet and keep warm.

Melt remaining 4 tblsp. butter in same skillet, about 2 minutes.

Add mushrooms, onion and garlic. Sauté 10 minutes or until tender.

Add paprika, salt, pepper, beef bouillon granules, ketchup, Worcestershire sauce and beef strips.

Combine flour and water in jar. Cover and shake until blended. Add flour mixture to skillet. Cook, stirring constantly, until mixture boils and thickens, about 3 minutes. Reduce heat to low (260⁰).

Stir some of the hot mixture into sour cream. Then stir sour cream mixture into skillet. Heat thoroughly, about 1 minute. (Do not boil.)

Serve over hot noodles. Garnish with chopped parsley.

Makes 4 servings.

168/Steak
with sour cream gravy

- *Preparation time: 25 minutes*
- *Cooking time: 1 hour 55 minutes*

A Swiss steak type of dish without the tomatoes—a nice break from the ordinary. It's also good served over fluffy rice.

3 lb. beef round steak,
  ½" thick
½ c. flour
1 tblsp. paprika
2 tsp. salt
½ c. cooking oil
1 c. sliced onion
½ lb. fresh mushrooms,
  sliced

1 clove garlic, minced
1½ c. water
1 c. dairy sour cream
2 tblsp. chopped fresh
  parsley
Hot mashed potatoes

Cut and measure all ingredients before starting to cook.

Pound steak with meat mallet to about ¼" thickness. Cut into serving pieces. Combine flour, paprika and salt. Dredge meat in flour mixture.

Heat ¼ c. of the oil in 12" skillet or electric frypan over medium heat (350⁰) 5 minutes or until hot.

Brown steak on both sides in hot oil, about 12 minutes, adding remaining ¼ c. oil as needed. Remove meat from skillet as it browns.

Add onion, mushrooms and garlic. Sauté 4 minutes. Stir in flour mixture if any is left. Slowly stir in water. Return meat to skillet. Cook until mixture comes to a boil, about 2 minutes.

Reduce heat to low (220⁰). Cover and simmer 1½ hours or until meat is tender.

Remove meat to platter and keep warm. Stir some of the hot gravy into sour cream. Then stir sour cream mixture into skillet. Heat about 2 minutes. (Do not boil.) Spoon some of the gravy over meat; garnish with parsley. Pour remaining gravy into a serving bowl. Serve with mashed potatoes.

Makes 8 to 10 servings.

169/Hellenic-style stew

• *Preparation time: 14 minutes*
• *Cooking time: 1 hour 32 minutes*

This stew is so different that it's perfect for dinner guests. The whole cloves, cinnamon stick and allspice make it unique.

¼ c. cooking oil
2 lb. beef round steak, cut into 2 × ¾" strips
2½ c. sliced onion, ¼" thick
2 large green peppers, cut into strips
2 cloves garlic, minced
2½ c. water
¼ c. vinegar
1 tblsp. brown sugar, packed
2 tsp. salt

¼ tsp. pepper
1 bay leaf
10 whole cloves
1 (1") cinnamon stick
½ tsp. ground allspice
1 (6-oz.) can tomato paste
1¼ lb. potatoes, pared and cut into eighths
½ lb. fresh small mushrooms
2 tblsp. flour
½ c. water

Cut and measure all ingredients before starting to cook.

Heat oil in 12" skillet or electric frypan over medium heat (350⁰) 5 minutes or until hot.

Add beef strips and cook 6 minutes or until well browned. Add onion, green pepper strips, garlic, 2½ c. water, vinegar, brown sugar, salt, pepper, bay leaf, cloves, cinnamon stick, allspice and tomato paste. Cook until mixture comes to a boil, about 4 minutes.

Reduce heat to low (220⁰). Cover and simmer 45 minutes.

Add potatoes and mushrooms. Cover and simmer 30 minutes.

Remove bay leaf, cinnamon stick and cloves. Combine flour and ½ c. water in jar. Cover and shake until blended. Stir flour mixture into stew. Cook, stirring constantly, until mixture boils and thickens, about 2 minutes.

Makes 6 servings.

170/Swiss steak elegante

• Preparation time: 12 minutes
• Cooking time: 1 hour 6 minutes

Here's a recipe developed with meat-and-potato fans in mind—there's lots of gravy to spoon over mashed potatoes or rice.

2 lb. beef round steak, ½" thick	1 (4-oz.) can mushroom stems and pieces, drained
¼ c. flour	1 clove garlic, minced
1 tblsp. paprika	½ c. water
1 tsp. salt	1 tblsp. flour
¼ tsp. pepper	2 tblsp. water
3 tblsp. cooking oil	½ c. dairy sour cream
¼ c. chopped onion	

Cut and measure all ingredients before starting to cook.

Cut round steak into 6 serving pieces. Tenderize steak by pounding on both sides with a meat mallet.

Combine ¼ c. flour, paprika, salt and pepper. Dredge steak in flour mixture.

Heat oil in 12" skillet or electric frypan over medium heat (350⁰) 5 minutes or until hot.

Brown floured steak on both sides in hot oil, about 10 minutes. Pour off excess fat.

Add onion, mushrooms, garlic and ½ c. water. Cook until mixture comes to a boil, about 1 minute.

Reduce heat to low (220⁰). Cover and simmer 45 minutes or until steak is tender.

Remove meat to platter and keep warm. Combine 1 tblsp. flour and 2 tblsp. water in jar. Cover and shake until blended.

Stir flour mixture into hot pan juices. Cook, stirring constantly, until mixture boils and thickens, about 3 minutes. Blend in sour cream. Heat, but do not let boil, about 2 minutes. Pour over steak. Serve with mashed potatoes, if you wish.

Makes 6 servings.

171/Enchilada casserole

- *Preparation time: 10 minutes*
- *Cooking time: 17 minutes*

This Mexican-style main dish is a great choice for casual dining. Round out the menu with a crisp green salad and corn bread.

3 tblsp. cooking oil
8 corn tortillas
1 lb. ground beef
¼ c. chopped onion
1 (16-oz.) can refried
  beans
¼ c. hot taco sauce
½ tsp. salt

Dash of garlic powder
⅓ c. sliced pitted ripe
  olives
1 (10-oz.) can enchilada
  sauce
1½ c. shredded Cheddar
  cheese

Cut and measure all ingredients before starting to cook.

Preheat 12″ skillet or electric frypan over low heat (220°) 2 minutes or until hot.

Add oil. Dip tortillas into hot oil on both sides to soften. Remove and set aside. (Total cooking time: 3 minutes.)

Increase heat to medium (350°).

Cook ground beef and onion in oil 5 minutes or until browned. Transfer mixture to bowl. Turn off heat.

Pour off fat from skillet.

Stir refried beans, taco sauce, salt and garlic powder into meat mixture. Stir in olives. Place a generous ⅓ c. meat mixture on each tortilla and roll up.

Pour enchilada sauce into same skillet. Roll filled tortillas in sauce to moisten all sides. Place all the tortillas in sauce, seam side down. Cover and place over low heat (220°).

When mixture begins to simmer, cover and cook 5 minutes. Spoon sauce over tortillas. Sprinkle with Cheddar cheese. Cover and cook 2 minutes more or until cheese melts.

Makes 4 servings.

172/Swedish meatballs with noodles

• Preparation time: 21 minutes
• Cooking time: 28 minutes

This recipe makes 48 tiny, well-seasoned meatballs which simmer in a delicate sour cream sauce. Attractive with parsley garnish.

1½ lb. ground chuck
¾ c. soft bread crumbs
⅓ c. finely chopped onion
3 tblsp. chopped fresh
  parsley
1 egg, beaten
1 tsp. salt
¼ tsp. ground allspice
⅛ tsp. pepper
⅛ tsp. ground nutmeg
½ c. milk
¼ c. cooking oil

¼ c. flour
½ tsp. paprika
⅛ tsp. pepper
1 (10½-oz.) can condensed
  beef broth
¾ c. water
1 c. dairy sour cream
8 oz. wide noodles, cooked
  and drained
2 tblsp. chopped fresh
  parsley

Cut and measure all ingredients before starting to cook.

Combine ground chuck, bread crumbs, onion, 3 tblsp. parsley, egg, salt, allspice, ⅛ tsp. pepper, nutmeg and milk in bowl. Mix lightly, but well. Shape mixture into 48 meatballs.

Heat oil in 12″ skillet or electric frypan over medium heat (350⁰) 5 minutes or until hot. Brown meatballs in oil, about 8 minutes. Remove and drain on paper towels. Keep warm.

Drain off all but ¼ c. fat from skillet. Stir flour, paprika and ⅛ tsp. pepper into fat. Cook over medium heat (350⁰) 1 minute. Slowly stir in beef broth and water. Cook, stirring constantly, until mixture boils and thickens, about 2 minutes.

Add meatballs. Reduce heat to low (220⁰). Cover and simmer 10 minutes. Remove from heat. Stir some of hot gravy into sour cream. Then stir sour cream mixture into skillet. Stir in noodles and heat thoroughly, about 2 minutes. Sprinkle with 2 tblsp. parsley before serving.

Makes 6 servings.

173/Eggplant-rice skillet

• *Preparation time: 15 minutes*
• *Cooking time: 45 minutes*

An easy dish that gently simmers with very little attention from the hostess, leaving her lots of time to chat with guests.

1½ lb. ground beef
1 c. chopped onion
1 clove garlic, minced
1 (16-oz.) can tomatoes, cut up
2 tsp. salt
1 tsp. dried oregano leaves

⅛ tsp. pepper
1 lb. eggplant, pared and cubed (4¼ c.)
1 c. water
1 c. quick-cooking rice
½ c. shredded mozzarella cheese

Cut and measure all ingredients before starting to cook.

Cook ground beef, onion and garlic in 12″ skillet or electric frypan over medium heat (350⁰) 10 minutes or until well browned. Drain off excess fat.

Stir in tomatoes, salt, oregano, pepper, eggplant and water. Cook until mixture comes to a boil, about 2 minutes. Stir in rice.

Reduce heat to low (220⁰). Cover and simmer 30 minutes or until eggplant and rice are tender. Stir occasionally while mixture is cooking.

Sprinkle with cheese. Cover and cook 3 minutes or until cheese melts.

Makes 6 servings.

174/Dill beef rolls

- *Preparation time: 16 minutes*
- *Cooking time: 39 minutes*

"I often bring this to potluck suppers," wrote a Wisconsin woman. "Everyone compliments me and it's usually gone in a hurry."

1½ lb. ground chuck
1 c. soft bread crumbs
1 c. beef broth
1 egg, slightly beaten
1 tsp. dry mustard
¼ tsp. salt
2 dill pickles, cut
lengthwise into sixths

2 tblsp. cooking oil
¼ c. dill pickle juice
1 (10¾-oz.) can condensed
cream of mushroom
soup
4 c. hot cooked rice
Chopped fresh parsley

Cut and measure all ingredients before starting to cook.

Combine ground chuck, bread crumbs, beef broth, egg, mustard and salt in bowl. Mix lightly, but well. Divide mixture into 12 equal portions. Shape each portion into a roll around each piece of dill pickle, covering pickle completely.

Heat oil in 12″ skillet or electric frypan over medium heat (350⁰) 5 minutes or until hot.

Brown 6 meat rolls at a time in hot oil, about 6 minutes. Remove meat rolls. Repeat with remaining meat rolls, about 6 minutes. Remove meat rolls.

Pour off all fat from skillet. Mix together pickle juice and mushroom soup in same skillet. Add meat rolls. Place over medium heat (350⁰) and cook until mixture comes to a boil, about 2 minutes.

Reduce heat to low (220⁰). Cover and simmer 20 minutes, basting rolls twice.

Serve on hot cooked rice. Garnish with chopped parsley.

Makes 6 servings.

175/Polynesian meatballs

- *Preparation time: 20 minutes*
- *Cooking time: 19 minutes*

A colorful entrée developed by one of our test kitchen home economists featuring meatballs in piquant sweet-and-sour sauce.

1½ lb. ground chuck
¾ c. soft bread crumbs
1 clove garlic, minced
¼ c. finely chopped onion
2 eggs, beaten
¼ c. milk
½ tsp. salt
¼ tsp. ground ginger
2 tsp. soy sauce
⅛ tsp. pepper
¼ c. cooking oil

1 (20-oz.) can pineapple chunks in juice
1 large green pepper, cut into strips
⅓ c. brown sugar, packed
½ c. vinegar
2 tblsp. soy sauce
3 tblsp. cornstarch
1 c. water
Hot cooked rice

Cut and measure all ingredients before starting to cook.

Combine ground chuck, bread crumbs, garlic, onion, eggs, milk, salt, ginger, 2 tsp. soy sauce and pepper in bowl. Mix lightly, but well. Shape mixture into 48 meatballs.

Heat oil in 12″ skillet or electric frypan over medium heat (350⁰) 5 minutes or until hot.

Brown meatballs on all sides in hot oil, about 8 minutes. Remove meatballs from skillet and drain on paper towels. Drain off fat from skillet.

Combine undrained pineapple, green pepper, brown sugar, vinegar and 2 tblsp. soy sauce in skillet. Cook over medium heat (350⁰), stirring constantly, until mixture comes to a boil, about 1 minute. Reduce heat to low (220⁰). Cover and simmer 3 minutes. Add meatballs.

Combine cornstarch and water in small bowl; stir until blended. Stir cornstarch mixture into skillet. Cook until mixture boils and thickens, about 2 minutes.

Serve with cooked rice.

Makes 6 servings.

176/Skillet moussaka

- *Preparation time: 18 minutes*
- *Cooking time: 58 minutes*

This American version of a classic Greek dish can be made with either ground chuck or ground lamb.

1 lb. ground chuck
¾ c. chopped onion
¼ c. ketchup
½ c. beef broth
1 tsp. salt
⅛ tsp. pepper
⅛ tsp. ground nutmeg
2 tblsp. chopped fresh parsley
4 tblsp. cooking oil
1½ lb. eggplant, pared and cut into ¼" slices

¼ c. butter or regular margarine
¼ c. flour
¼ tsp. salt
⅛ tsp. ground nutmeg
2 c. milk
2 eggs, separated
½ c. soft bread crumbs
½ c. grated Parmesan cheese

Cut and measure all ingredients before starting to cook.

Cook ground chuck and onion in 12″ skillet or electric frypan over medium heat (350⁰) 5 minutes or until browned.

Add the next 6 ingredients. Reduce heat to low (220⁰). Simmer 10 minutes. Remove meat mixture from skillet.

Heat 1 tblsp. of the oil in skillet over medium heat (350⁰) 1 minute. Fry eggplant 2 minutes on each side. Add 2 tblsp. more oil as needed. (Total cooking time: 15 minutes.)

Melt butter in skillet over medium heat (350⁰), about 2 minutes. Stir in flour, ¼ tsp. salt and ⅛ tsp. nutmeg. Slowly stir in milk. Cook, stirring, until it boils, about 3 minutes. Turn off heat. Stir some of the hot sauce into yolks. Then stir yolk mixture into skillet. Pour into a bowl.

Beat egg whites until stiff. Fold in bread crumbs. Stir into meat mixture. Heat remaining 1 tblsp. oil in skillet. Turn heat to low (220⁰). Layer one half of eggplant in skillet. Top with meat mixture and then remaining eggplant. Pour sauce over all; sprinkle with cheese. Cover and cook 20 minutes.

Makes 6 servings.

177/Veal Parmesan

- *Preparation time: 16 minutes*
- *Cooking time: 1 hour 2 minutes*

Succulent pieces of veal cutlet simmer in a mildly spicy tomato sauce. The sauce is extra-thick and rich.

2 tblsp. cooking oil
½ lb. fresh mushrooms, sliced
1 c. chopped onion
2 cloves garlic, minced
¾ c. water
1 (28-oz.) can Italian tomatoes, puréed in blender
1 (6-oz.) can tomato paste
1 tsp. salt
¾ tsp. dried basil leaves

⅛ tsp. pepper
½ c. soft bread crumbs
½ c. grated Parmesan cheese
1 lb. thinly sliced veal cutlets
2 eggs, slightly beaten
¼ c. cooking oil
½ c. grated Parmesan cheese
8 oz. noodles, cooked and drained

Cut and measure all ingredients before starting to cook.

Heat 2 tblsp. oil in 12″ skillet or electric frypan over medium heat (325⁰) 5 minutes or until hot.

Add mushrooms, onion and garlic. Sauté 10 minutes or until tender. Add water, puréed tomatoes, tomato paste, salt, basil and pepper. Cook until it comes to a boil, about 2 minutes. Reduce heat to low (220⁰). Simmer, partially covered, 15 minutes. Remove sauce from skillet. Wash out skillet.

Combine bread crumbs and ½ c. Parmesan cheese. Dip veal into beaten egg and then coat with crumb mixture. Heat ¼ c. oil in skillet over medium heat (350⁰) 5 minutes or until hot.

Brown breaded veal cutlets on both sides in hot oil, about 5 minutes. Pour sauce over veal cutlets. Cover and cook over low heat (220⁰) 10 minutes.

Sprinkle with ½ c. Parmesan cheese. Cover and simmer 10 minutes more. Arrange noodles on platter. Spoon sauce over noodles and arrange veal cutlets on top.

Makes 4 servings.

178/Spanish pork chops

- *Preparation time: 16 minutes*
- *Cooking time: 1 hour 7 minutes*

These chops stay extra-moist during cooking when simmered with green pepper and tomatoes on top of the garlic-scented rice.

6 strips bacon, diced	**2 (16-oz.) cans tomatoes,**
6 pork chops, ¾″ thick	**cut up**
¾ c. chopped onion	**1½ tsp. salt**
½ c. chopped green pepper	**½ tsp. paprika**
½ c. sliced celery, ⅛″ thick	**⅛ tsp. pepper**
½ lb. fresh mushrooms,	**1 bay leaf**
sliced	**1 chicken bouillon cube**
1 clove garlic, minced	**1 c. uncooked regular rice**

Cut and measure all ingredients before starting to cook.

Fry bacon in 12″ skillet or electric frypan over medium heat (350⁰) until browned, about 6 minutes.

Pour off bacon drippings, reserving 2 tblsp. Return 2 tblsp. bacon drippings to same skillet. Brown pork chops on both sides, about 12 minutes. Remove from skillet.

Add onion, green pepper, celery, mushrooms and garlic to skillet. Saute 7 minutes or until tender.

Stir in tomatoes, salt, paprika, pepper, bay leaf and bouillon cube. Arrange pork chops on top. Cook until mixture comes to a boil, about 2 minutes.

Reduce heat to low (220⁰). Cover and simmer 10 minutes.

Remove chops. Stir in rice. Replace chops. Cover and cook 15 minutes. Turn chops over and stir rice mixture. Cover and simmer 15 minutes more or until pork chops and rice are tender.

Makes 6 servings.

179/Pork steaks with mushroom gravy

• Preparation time: 6 minutes
• Cooking time: 1 hour 24 minutes

Loin or rib pork chops can be used instead of pork steaks for a more special main dish. Good for a family Sunday dinner, too.

6 lean pork steaks,
  ¾" thick (2½ lb.)
½ tsp. salt
¼ tsp. pepper
2 tblsp. cooking oil
½ c. chopped onion
1 (8-oz.) can sliced
  mushrooms

1 (10½-oz.) can condensed
  beef broth
1 tsp. Worcestershire
  sauce
1 c. evaporated milk
1 tblsp. flour

Cut and measure all ingredients before starting to cook.

Season pork steaks with salt and pepper.

Heat oil in 12" skillet or electric frypan over medium heat (350⁰) 5 minutes or until hot.

Brown pork steaks on both sides in hot oil, about 10 minutes. Remove from skillet. Add onion and sauté 3 minutes.

Drain mushrooms, reserving liquid. Add reserved liquid, beef broth, Worcestershire sauce and pork steaks to skillet. Cook until mixture comes to a boil, about 2 minutes.

Reduce heat to low (220⁰). Cover and simmer 1 hour or until pork steaks are tender.

Remove pork steaks to platter and keep warm.

Add mushrooms to skillet. Turn heat to medium (350⁰). Cook until mixture comes to a boil, about 1 minute. Combine evaporated milk and flour in a jar. Cover and shake until blended. Stir flour mixture into skillet. Cook, stirring constantly, until mixture thickens, about 3 minutes. (Do not boil.) Serve gravy with pork steaks.

Makes 6 servings.

180/French-style bean casserole

- *Preparation time: 11 minutes*
- *Cooking time: 1 hour 20 minutes*

This is a skillet version of the classic French cassoulet featuring herb-seasoned white beans with pork, bacon and smoked sausage.

½ lb. bacon, diced
6 pork chops, ¾" thick
  (about 2 lb.)
1½ c. chopped onion
2 cloves garlic, minced
2 (15-oz.) cans Great
  Northern beans, drained
1 (6-oz.) can tomato paste

½ c. white vermouth
½ tsp. dried thyme leaves
2 bay leaves
⅛ tsp. pepper
1 lb. Kielbasa or smoked
  pork sausage, cut into
  ½" slices

Cut and measure all ingredients before starting to cook.

Fry bacon in 12" skillet or electric frypan over medium heat (350°) 8 minutes or until browned. Remove bacon with slotted spoon and drain on paper towels.

Brown pork chops in bacon drippings over medium heat (350°), about 8 minutes. Remove pork chops.

Stir in onion and garlic. Saute 2 minutes or until tender. Stir in beans, tomato paste, vermouth, thyme, bay leaves, pepper, Kielbasa and bacon. Top with pork chops. Cook until mixture comes to a boil, about 2 minutes.

Reduce heat to low (220°). Cover and simmer 1 hour or until pork is tender.

Makes 6 servings.

181/Sweet-sour spareribs

• *Preparation time: 4 minutes*
• *Cooking time: 1 hour 7 minutes*

Plan a Hawaiian meal around these sweet-and-sour-sauced ribs. Since they're cooked in a skillet, your kitchen will stay cool.

3 lb. pork spareribs, cut
   into single ribs
3 c. water
1 (8-oz.) can pineapple
   chunks in juice
2 tblsp. cooking oil
1½ c. green pepper strips
1 c. sliced onions

1 clove garlic, minced
6 tblsp. sugar
3 tblsp. cornstarch
½ c. vinegar
2 tblsp. soy sauce
2 tblsp. ketchup
2 tblsp. cooking oil

Cut and measure all ingredients before starting to cook.
Place spareribs and water in 12″ skillet or electric frypan.
Cover and place over medium heat (350⁰). Bring to a boil, about 5 minutes. Reduce heat to low (220⁰). Simmer 25 minutes or until tender. Remove ribs and cool 15 minutes. Drain pineapple, reserving juice. Add enough water to juice to make 1½ c. Heat 2 tblsp. oil in same skillet over medium heat (350⁰), about 2 minutes. Add green pepper, onion and garlic. Sauté 2 minutes. Stir in 1½ c. liquid and bring to a boil, about 1 minute. Reduce heat to low (220⁰). Cover and simmer 3 minutes.

Combine sugar, cornstarch, vinegar, soy sauce and ketchup in a bowl. Stir into skillet. Add pineapple. Cook, stirring, until it boils and thickens, about 3 minutes. Pour into bowl.

Heat 2 tblsp. oil in same skillet over medium heat (325⁰) 3 minutes. Brown spareribs in oil, about 6 minutes. Pour sauce over ribs and heat 2 minutes, coating well with sauce.

Makes 4 servings.

182/Ham and broccoli royale

• Preparation time: 15 minutes
• Cooking time: 41 minutes

This ham dish layered with broccoli spears and fluffy rice in a cheese sauce is a good choice for a buffet supper—it serves eight.

4 c. water
1½ lb. fresh broccoli, cut into flowerets
6 tblsp. butter or regular margarine
2 c. soft bread crumbs
2 c. chopped onion
3 tblsp. flour

¼ tsp. pepper
3 c. milk
4 c. cubed fully cooked ham
2 c. cooked regular rice
1 (8-oz.) pkg. sliced process American cheese

Cut and measure all ingredients before starting to cook.

Heat water in 12″ skillet or electric frypan over high heat (420⁰) until it comes to a boil, about 5 minutes.

Add broccoli. Reduce heat to low (220⁰). Cover and simmer 15 minutes or until broccoli is tender. Drain in colander.

Melt butter in same skillet over medium heat (300⁰), about 3 minutes. Remove 2 tblsp. of the butter and mix with bread crumbs. Set aside.

Add onion to melted butter in skillet. Sauté 2 minutes. Stir in flour and pepper. Gradually stir in milk. Cook, stirring constantly, until mixture boils and thickens, about 4 minutes. Add ham and cook 2 minutes. Pour ham mixture into a bowl.

Spoon rice evenly in bottom of same skillet. Arrange broccoli in layer on top. Pour ham mixture over all. Arrange cheese on top. Sprinkle with buttered bread crumbs.

Place over low heat (220⁰). Cover and simmer 10 minutes or until thoroughly heated.

Makes 8 servings.

183/Ham and cauliflower chowder

• Preparation time: 13 minutes
• Cooking time: 44 minutes

A rich and creamy soup so thick it's chowder-like. Add a basket of crusty rolls and fresh salad greens to make it a meal.

2 c. water
½ tsp. salt
1½ lb. cauliflower, cut into flowerets (about 4 c.)
¼ c. butter or regular margarine
½ c. chopped onion
¼ c. flour

⅛ tsp. dry mustard
¹⁄₁₆ tsp. pepper
3½ c. milk
2 c. shredded Cheddar cheese
1 lb. fully cooked ham, cut into 1″ strips
¼ c. chopped fresh parsley

Cut and measure all ingredients before starting to cook.

Heat water and salt in 12″ skillet or electric frypan over high heat (400⁰) or until it comes to a boil, about 3 minutes.

Add cauliflower and return to a boil. Cook 5 minutes. Cover and cook 5 minutes more.

Drain cauliflower in colander. Wipe out skillet.

Melt butter in same skillet over medium heat (300⁰), about 2 minutes. Add onion and sauté 4 minutes or until tender.

Stir in flour, mustard and pepper. Gradually stir in milk. Cook, stirring constantly, until mixture boils and thickens, about 10 minutes.

Stir in cheese. Then add ham and cauliflower. Reduce heat to low (220⁰). Heat 15 minutes. Garnish with chopped parsley.

Makes about 1 quart.

184/Carbonara

- *Preparation time: 7 minutes*
- *Cooking time: 14 minutes*

This extra-fast ham and spaghetti dish is pretty enough to serve right from the skillet.

4 strips bacon, diced	**2 eggs, beaten**
2 tblsp. butter or regular margarine	**⅓ c. grated Parmesan cheese**
¼ lb. fully cooked ham, cut into 2″ julienne strips	**¼ tsp. salt**
	¼ tsp. pepper
8 oz. spaghetti, cooked and drained	**3 tblsp. chopped fresh parsley**
	Grated Parmesan cheese

Cut and measure all ingredients before starting to cook.

Fry bacon in 12″ skillet or electric frypan over medium heat (350⁰) 10 minutes or until browned. Remove with slotted spoon and drain on paper towels. Pour off fat from skillet.

Melt butter in same skillet over medium heat (300⁰), about 1 minute. Add ham and sauté 3 minutes. Turn off heat.

Add hot cooked spaghetti, eggs, ⅓ c. Parmesan cheese, salt, pepper and parsley. Toss quickly to coat spaghetti.

Arrange on warm platter and sprinkle with Parmesan cheese.

Makes 4 servings.

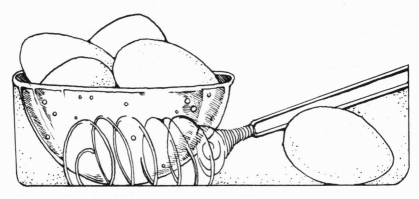

FARM JOURNAL'S SPEEDY SKILLET MEALS

185/Chicken with rosemary

• *Preparation time: 10 minutes*
• *Cooking time: 49 minutes*

Egg yolks and cream make the sauce extra-rich. As an accompaniment, toss some fresh chopped parsley into fluffy rice.

½ c. flour
½ tsp. salt
⅛ tsp. pepper
1 (3-lb.) broiler-fryer,
  cut up
¼ c. butter or regular
  margarine
1 chicken bouillon cube
1 c. boiling water

1 tsp. dried rosemary
  leaves
½ tsp. dried thyme leaves
1 clove garlic, minced
1 bay leaf
1 c. heavy cream
4 egg yolks, beaten
¼ tsp. salt

Cut and measure all ingredients before starting to cook.

Combine flour, ½ tsp. salt and pepper. Dredge chicken in flour mixture.

Melt butter in 12″ skillet or electric frypan over medium heat (350⁰), about 3 minutes.

Brown chicken on all sides in melted butter, about 10 minutes.

Dissolve chicken bouillon cube in boiling water; stir well.

Add chicken bouillon, rosemary, thyme, garlic and bay leaf to chicken. Cook until mixture comes to a boil, about 3 minutes.

Reduce heat to low (220⁰). Cover and simmer 30 minutes or until chicken is tender.

Arrange chicken on platter and keep warm. Combine heavy cream, egg yolks and ¼ tsp. salt in bowl; stir well. Stir mixture into pan drippings. Cook over low heat (220⁰), stirring constantly, until mixture is thickened, about 3 minutes. (Do not boil.) Pour sauce over chicken.

Makes 4 servings.

186/Chicken breasts stuffed with beef

- *Preparation time: 25 minutes*
- *Cooking time: 47 minutes*

Here are two country-style foods combined in a different way—special enough for company and such a snap to prepare.

¼ c. butter or regular margarine
3 whole chicken breasts, split
½ c. chopped onion
2 oz. dried beef
1 tblsp. flour
½ tsp. dried basil leaves
¼ tsp. salt

⅛ tsp. ground nutmeg
⅛ tsp. pepper
1 (8¾-oz.) can whole-kernel corn
⅓ c. milk
1½ c. dairy sour cream
2 tblsp. chopped pimientos
1 tblsp. minced fresh parsley

Cut and measure all ingredients before starting to cook.

Melt butter in 12″ skillet or electric frypan over medium heat (350⁰), about 3 minutes.

Brown chicken on all sides in melted butter, about 10 minutes. Sprinkle with onion. Reduce heat to low (220⁰). Cover and simmer 25 minutes or until chicken is tender.

Remove chicken from skillet and let cool until it can be easily handled. Reserve pan drippings; set aside.

Place dried beef in a sieve and rinse with hot water. Drain well and chop finely. Make lengthwise slit in thickest part of each breast with knife. Stuff with one sixth of the dried beef.

Add flour, basil, salt, nutmeg and pepper to pan drippings in same skillet. Cook over medium heat (350⁰), stirring constantly, 1 minute. Add undrained corn and milk. Cook until it comes to a boil, about 2 minutes. Simmer 1 minute.

Stir some of the hot mixture into sour cream. Then stir sour cream mixture into skillet. Add pimientos and chicken breasts. Cover and cook over low heat (220⁰) 5 minutes.

Serve garnished with parsley.

Makes 6 servings.

187/Chicken with mushroom sauce

• Preparation time: 12 minutes
• Cooking time: 1 hour 12 minutes

This delicate chicken dish tastes even better with a chilled bottle of white chablis. Serve with peas and buttered noodles.

⅓ c. flour
¾ tsp. salt
¼ tsp. pepper
1 (3-lb.) broiler-fryer, cut up
¼ c. cooking oil
½ lb. fresh mushrooms, sliced
⅓ c. chopped green onions

½ tsp. minced garlic
1 chicken bouillon cube
½ c. boiling water
1 (8-oz.) can tomato sauce
¼ c. dry white wine
1 bay leaf
¼ tsp. dried thyme leaves
1 tblsp. flour
2 tblsp. water

Cut and measure all ingredients before starting to cook.

Combine ⅓ c. flour, salt and pepper. Dredge chicken in flour mixture. Reserve remaining flour mixture.

Heat oil in 12″ skillet or electric frypan over medium heat (350⁰) 5 minutes or until hot. Brown chicken on all sides in hot oil, about 10 minutes. Remove chicken as it browns.

Add mushrooms to pan drippings. Sauté 5 minutes. Add green onions and garlic; sauté 1 minute more.

Dissolve chicken bouillon cube in ½ c. water. Add chicken bouillon, tomato sauce, wine, bay leaf, thyme and chicken to skillet. Cook until mixture comes to a boil, about 3 minutes.

Reduce heat to low (220⁰). Cover and simmer 45 minutes or until chicken is tender.

Arrange chicken on platter and keep warm. Combine reserved flour mixture, 1 tblsp. flour and 2 tblsp. water in jar. Cover and shake until blended. Stir flour mixture into skillet. Cook until it comes to a boil, stirring constantly, about 2 minutes. Boil 1 minute. Spoon sauce over chicken.

Makes 4 servings.

COMPANY-PLEASING SPECIALTIES

188/Orange-glazed chicken

- *Preparation time: 10 minutes*
- *Cooking time: 50 minutes*

Simmered in orange juice, spiced with a hint of ginger and garnished with toasted almonds to give it a crunchy texture.

1 (3-lb.) broiler-fryer,
  cut up
1 tsp. salt
¼ c. cooking oil
¾ c. orange juice
1 tsp. instant minced onion
¼ tsp. ground ginger

⅛ tsp. Tabasco sauce
2 tsp. cornstarch
1 tblsp. water
¼ c. toasted slivered
  almonds
1 large orange, cut into
  sections

Cut and measure all ingredients before starting to cook.
Season chicken with salt.

Heat oil in 12″ skillet or electric frypan over medium heat (350⁰) 5 minutes or until hot.

Brown chicken on all sides in hot oil, about 10 minutes. Add orange juice, minced onion, ginger and Tabasco sauce. Cook until mixture comes to a boil, about 2 minutes.

Reduce heat to low (220⁰). Cover and simmer 30 minutes or until chicken is tender.

Arrange chicken on platter and keep warm. Combine cornstarch and water in small bowl; blend well. Stir cornstarch mixture into skillet. Cook until it comes to a boil, about 2 minutes. Boil 1 minute. Add almonds and orange sections. Spoon sauce over chicken.

Makes 4 servings.

189/Chicken breasts in heavy cream

- *Preparation time: 10 minutes*
- *Cooking time: 52 minutes*

You can omit the vermouth from this recipe if you wish. Just add a little water or chicken broth instead.

½ c. flour
½ tsp. salt
¼ tsp. pepper
3 whole chicken breasts, split
¼ c. butter or regular margarine
1 tblsp. butter or regular margarine
½ lb. fresh mushrooms, sliced

⅓ c. chopped onion
1 tblsp. flour
1½ tsp. paprika
½ tsp. salt
⅛ tsp. pepper
1 c. heavy cream
3 tblsp. dry vermouth
Fresh parsley sprigs

Cut and measure all ingredients before starting to cook.

Combine ½ c. flour, ½ tsp. salt and ¼ tsp. pepper. Dredge chicken breasts in flour mixture.

Melt ¼ c. butter in 12″ skillet or electric frypan over medium heat (350⁰), about 3 minutes.

Brown chicken on all sides in melted butter, about 10 minutes.

Reduce heat to low (220⁰). Cover and simmer 30 minutes or until chicken is tender.

Arrange chicken on platter and keep warm. Add 1 tblsp. butter to pan drippings and place over medium heat (350⁰). Add mushrooms and onion. Sauté 5 minutes.

Stir in 1 tblsp. flour, paprika, ½ tsp. salt and ⅛ tsp. pepper. Cook, stirring constantly, 1 minute. Gradually stir in heavy cream and vermouth. Cook over low heat (220⁰), stirring constantly, until thickened, about 3 minutes. (Do not boil.) Pour sauce over chicken. Garnish with parsley sprigs.

Makes 6 servings.

190/Summer chicken with peas

- *Preparation time: 10 minutes*
- *Cooking time: 55 minutes*

This is a favorite Farm Journal recipe that has been requested by our readers many times. You'll know why if you try it.

6 tblsp. butter or regular margarine	Pepper
1 (2½-lb.) broiler-fryer, cut up	3 green onions and tops, thinly sliced
1 lb. small new potatoes, scrubbed, with a strip peeled around center	1 (10-oz.) pkg. frozen peas
	¼ c. chopped fresh parsley
2 tblsp. lemon juice	1 c. dairy sour cream
Salt	1 tsp. dried thyme leaves
	½ tsp. salt
	¼ tsp. pepper

Cut and measure all ingredients before starting to cook.

Melt butter in 12″ skillet or electric frypan over medium heat (350⁰), about 3 minutes.

Brown chicken and potatoes on all sides in butter, about 10 minutes. Season chicken and potatoes with lemon juice, salt and pepper. Cover and simmer 30 minutes.

Add green onions to butter in bottom of skillet. Sprinkle peas and parsley over chicken and potatoes. Cover and simmer 10 minutes more or until chicken and potatoes are tender.

Remove chicken and vegetables to platter and keep warm. Remove skillet from heat. Add sour cream, thyme, ½ tsp. salt and ¼ tsp. pepper to skillet; stir well. Heat over low heat (220⁰) 2 minutes. (Do not boil.) Pour sauce over chicken and serve immediately.

Makes 4 servings.

191/Company chicken

• Preparation time: 20 minutes
• Cooking time: 25 minutes

A great buffet supper choice because it serves eight and is simple to prepare. Serve with a spinach salad and fresh fruit.

6 tblsp. butter or regular margarine
½ lb. fresh mushrooms, sliced
½ c. chopped onion
1 clove garlic, minced
5 tblsp. flour
1 tsp. salt
⅛ tsp. pepper
2 (10¾-oz.) cans condensed chicken broth

1 c. milk
¼ c. dry vermouth
3 c. cubed cooked chicken
8 oz. medium noodles, cooked and drained
¼ c. sliced pimiento-stuffed olives
2 tblsp. minced fresh parsley
½ c. grated Parmesan cheese

Cut and measure all ingredients before starting to cook.

Melt butter in 12″ skillet or electric frypan over medium heat (350⁰), about 3 minutes

Add mushrooms and onion to skillet. Sauté 8 minutes or until tender. Add garlic and sauté 1 minute.

Stir in flour, salt and pepper. Cook 1 minute, stirring constantly. Gradually stir in chicken broth, milk and vermouth. Cook, stirring constantly, until mixture boils and thickens, about 5 minutes.

Add chicken and noodles. Reduce heat to low (220⁰). Cover and simmer 5 minutes. Stir in olives and parsley. Sprinkle with Parmesan cheese. Cover and simmer 2 minutes more.

Makes 8 servings.

192/Mary's chicken in honey sauce

- *Preparation time: 5 minutes*
- *Cooking time: 55 minutes*

For a change of pace, add a little curry powder to rice while cooking—gives it a nice color and flavor. (See photo, Front Jacket.)

3 whole chicken breasts, split (about 3 lb.)
1 tsp. salt
¼ tsp. pepper
2 tblsp. cooking oil
1 (20-oz.) can pineapple chunks in juice
2 c. bias-cut pared carrots
⅓ c. chopped onion

1 c. water
½ c. cider vinegar
⅓ c. honey
1 tblsp. soy sauce
2 chicken bouillon cubes
¼ c. cornstarch
½ c. water
1 (6-oz.) pkg. frozen pea pods, thawed
Hot cooked rice

Cut and measure all ingredients before starting to cook.

Season chicken breasts with salt and pepper.

Heat oil in 12″ skillet or electric frypan over medium heat (350⁰) 5 minutes or until hot. Meanwhile, drain pineapple, reserving juice. Brown chicken in hot oil, about 10 minutes.

Stir in carrots, onion, 1 c. water, vinegar, honey, soy sauce, chicken bouillon cubes and reserved pineapple juice. Bring mixture to a boil, about 2 minutes.

Reduce heat to low (220⁰). Cover and simmer 35 minutes or until chicken is tender.

Remove chicken and keep warm. Combine cornstarch and ½ c. water in bowl; stir to blend. Stir cornstarch mixture into pan juices. Cook, stirring constantly, until mixture boils and thickens, about 2 minutes. Stir in pea pods and pineapple chunks. Cook 1 minute or until heated.

Arrange chicken on hot rice, placing vegetables in center. Spoon some of the sauce over chicken. Pass remaining sauce.

Makes 6 servings.

193/Malayan chicken

- *Preparation time: 5 minutes*
- *Cooking time: 49 minutes*

A delightful flavor combination: crunchy water chestnuts in an orange juice-wine sauce and spiced with ground ginger.

¼ c. cooking oil
1 (2½-lb.) broiler-fryer, cut up
½ c. orange juice
1 tsp. ground ginger
1 tsp. salt
⅛ tsp. garlic salt
1 (8-oz.) can pitted ripe olives, halved

1 (5¼-oz.) can water chestnuts, drained and sliced
1 c. dry white wine
2 tblsp. cornstarch
2 tblsp. water

Cut and measure all ingredients before starting to cook.

Heat oil in 10″ skillet over medium heat 3 minutes.

Brown chicken on all sides in hot oil, about 10 minutes.

Stir in orange juice, ginger, salt, garlic salt, olives, water chestnuts and wine. Cook until mixture comes to a boil, about 3 minutes.

Reduce heat to low. Cover and simmer 30 minutes or until chicken is tender. Arrange chicken on platter; keep warm.

Combine cornstarch and water in small bowl; stir until blended. Stir cornstarch mixture into pan juices. Cook, stirring constantly, until mixture boils and thickens, about 3 minutes. Pour sauce over chicken.

Makes 4 servings.

194/Chicken paprika

• *Preparation time: 25 minutes*
• *Cooking time: 1 hour*

You don't have to wait for a special occasion to serve this Hungarian-inspired dish—surprise your family next Sunday.

¼ c. flour
½ tsp. salt
¼ tsp. pepper
1 (3-lb.) broiler-fryer, cut up
⅓ c. cooking oil
3 c. sliced onion
1 tblsp. paprika

1 (10¾-oz.) can condensed chicken broth
6 medium carrots, pared and cut into strips
3 tblsp. flour
¼ c. water
1 c. dairy sour cream
Chopped fresh parsley

Cut and measure all ingredients before starting to cook.

Combine ¼ c. flour, salt and pepper. Dredge chicken in flour mixture.

Heat oil in 12″ skillet or electric frypan over medium heat (350º) 5 minutes or until hot.

Brown chicken on all sides in hot oil, about 10 minutes. Remove chicken as it browns.

Add onion to pan drippings. Sauté 5 minutes or until tender. Stir in paprika. Slowly stir in chicken broth. Cook until mixture comes to a boil, about 3 minutes.

Add chicken and carrots. Reduce heat to low (220º). Cover and simmer 30 minutes or until chicken is tender.

Arrange chicken and carrots on platter and keep warm. Combine 3 tblsp. flour and water in jar. Cover and shake until blended. Stir flour mixture into pan juices. Cook, stirring constantly, over medium heat (350º) 5 minutes or until mixture boils and thickens.

Remove from heat. Stir some of the hot mixture into sour cream. Then stir sour cream mixture into skillet. Heat over low heat 2 minutes. Pour ½ c. of the sauce over chicken. Serve remaining sauce with chicken. Sprinkle chicken with parsley.

Makes 4 servings.

195/Chicken cacciatore

- *Preparation time: 2 minutes*
- *Cooking time: 55 minutes*

If you keep the ingredients on hand, you can easily serve this popular Italian-inspired main dish on the spur of the moment.

¼ c. cooking oil
1 (3-lb.) broiler-fryer, cut up
1 (1½-oz.) pkg. spaghetti seasoning mix
1 (15-oz.) can tomato sauce
1 (4-oz.) can mushroom stems and pieces, drained
½ tsp. salt
⅛ tsp. pepper
8 oz. spaghetti, cooked and drained
Grated Parmesan cheese

Measure all ingredients before starting to cook.

Heat oil in 10″ skillet over medium heat 3 minutes or until hot.

Brown chicken on all sides in hot oil, about 10 minutes. Remove chicken from skillet. Pour off fat.

Combine spaghetti seasoning mix and tomato sauce in same skillet. Cook until mixture comes to a boil, about 2 minutes.

Add mushrooms, salt, pepper and chicken. Spoon sauce over chicken.

Reduce heat to low. Cover and simmer 40 minutes or until chicken is tender. Serve over hot spaghetti. Pass Parmesan cheese.

Makes 4 servings.

196/Chicken with spaghetti

• Preparation time: 8 minutes
• Cooking time: 29 minutes

You can prepare this Italian-inspired dish in less than an hour. Pass freshly grated Parmesan for an authentic touch.

½ c. cooking oil
½ c. butter or regular
   margarine
2 cloves garlic, minced
½ c. chopped fresh parsley

1 (13¾-oz.) can chicken
   broth
2 c. diced cooked chicken
8 oz. spaghetti or linguine,
   cooked and drained

Cut and measure all ingredients before starting to cook.

Heat oil and butter in 10″ skillet over medium heat until butter melts, about 5 minutes.

Add garlic and sauté 3 minutes. Add parsley and chicken broth. Cook until mixture comes to a boil, about 1 minute.

Reduce heat to low. Simmer, uncovered, 10 minutes.

Add chicken and simmer 10 minutes more.

Pour sauce over hot spaghetti and toss gently to mix. Makes 6 servings.

197/Sweet-and-sour fish

• *Preparation time: 12 minutes*
• *Cooking time: 30 minutes*

Serve golden brown and crispy fish fingers in a sweet-and-sour sauce flavored with pineapple chunks and green pepper.

1 (1-lb.) pkg. frozen
  haddock fillets, thawed
4 c. cooking oil
¼ c. flour
¼ c. cornstarch
4 tsp. water
1 egg, beaten
½ tsp. salt
1 c. green pepper strips
1 (8-oz.) can pineapple
  chunks in juice

Water
1½ tsp. chicken bouillon
  granules
2 tblsp. cornstarch
¼ c. sugar
2 tblsp. soy sauce
¼ c. vinegar
Hot cooked rice

Cut and measure all ingredients before starting to cook.

Don't separate haddock fillets. Cut block of haddock into 3 × 1″ strips. Heat oil in 12″ skillet or electric frypan over medium heat (365⁰) 6 minutes or until hot.

Combine flour, ¼ c. cornstarch, 4 tsp. water, egg and salt in bowl. Beat until smooth. Dip fish into batter, coating well. Fry 4 pieces of fish at a time in oil 7 minutes or until golden, turning occasionally. Remove and drain on paper towels. Repeat with remaining fish, frying 7 minutes more.

Remove all but 1 tblsp. of the oil from skillet. Heat over medium heat (325⁰) 1 minute. Add green pepper; sauté 2 minutes. Drain pineapple, reserving juice. Add enough water to pineapple juice to make 1½ c. Add 1½ c. pineapple liquid to skillet with bouillon granules. Cook until it boils, about 2 minutes.

Reduce heat to low (220⁰). Cover and simmer 3 minutes.

Combine 2 tblsp. cornstarch and sugar in bowl. Stir in soy sauce and vinegar. Add cornstarch mixture to skillet. Cook, stirring constantly, until mixture boils and thickens, about 2 minutes. Arrange fish on rice; pour sauce over all.

Makes 4 servings.

COMPANY-PLEASING SPECIALTIES

198/Squash and haddock chowder

- *Preparation time: 10 minutes*
- *Cooking time: 43 minutes*

Squash gives this unusual chowder a velvety texture. It's a delightful blend of haddock, lima beans and a hint of ginger.

1 (1-lb.) pkg. frozen
   haddock fillets, thawed
¼ c. butter or regular
   margarine
1 c. sliced celery, ⅛" thick
1 c. chopped onion
1 (10¾-oz.) can condensed
   chicken broth
1 (10-oz.) pkg. frozen
   Fordhook lima beans
2 c. milk

¾ tsp. salt
⅛ tsp. pepper
⅛ tsp. ground ginger
1 tblsp. Worcestershire
   sauce
¼ c. flour
½ c. water
1 (12-oz.) pkg. frozen
   cooked squash, thawed
Paprika

Cut and measure all ingredients before starting to cook.

Do not separate haddock fillets. Cut block of fish into 1" chunks and set aside.

Melt butter in 12" skillet or electric frypan over medium heat (350⁰), about 2 minutes. Add celery and onion. Sauté 7 minutes. Add chicken broth and lima beans and bring to a boil, about 4 minutes.

Reduce heat to low (220⁰). Cover and simmer 15 minutes.

Stir milk, salt, pepper, ginger and Worcestershire sauce into skillet. Combine flour and water in jar. Cover and shake until blended. Stir flour mixture into chowder. Cook over medium heat (350⁰), stirring constantly, until mixture thickens and boils, about 4 minutes.

Add squash and heat 3 minutes or until mixture returns to a boil. Add haddock. Reduce heat to low (250⁰) and simmer, uncovered, 8 minutes or until fish flakes easily. Sprinkle with paprika before serving.

Makes about 2 quarts.

199/Spanish shrimp with rice

- *Preparation time: 35 minutes*
- *Cooking time: 40 minutes*

Tender shrimp with clams and saffron-flavored rice make this one of the best skillet dishes we've ever tested.

1 tblsp. cooking oil
½ lb. Italian sweet
  sausage, cut into
  ¾" pieces
1 c. green pepper strips
½ c. sliced onion
2 cloves garlic, minced
1 (16-oz.) can tomatoes,
  cut up
1 (10-oz.) can whole baby
  clams

Chicken broth
1 c. uncooked regular rice
½ tsp. salt
⅛ tsp. powdered saffron
1 lb. medium raw shrimp,
  shelled and deveined
1 (10-oz.) pkg. frozen peas,
  thawed

Cut and measure all ingredients before starting to cook.

Heat oil in 12″ skillet or electric frypan over medium heat (300⁰) 5 minutes or until hot.

Add sausage, green pepper, onion and garlic. Sauté 8 minutes.

Drain tomatoes and clams, reserving juice. Add enough chicken broth to juice to make 2½ c.

Stir tomatoes, 2½ c. juice, rice, salt and saffron into skillet. Cook until mixture comes to a boil, about 2 minutes.

Reduce heat to low (220⁰). Cover and simmer 15 minutes.

Stir in shrimp. Cover and simmer 5 minutes.

Add clams and peas. Cover and simmer 5 minutes. Remove from heat and let stand 5 minutes before serving.

Makes 4 servings.

200/Tuna divan

- *Preparation time: 6 minutes*
- *Cooking time: 33 minutes*

We substituted tuna for chicken in this classic dish. It's lightly spiced with nutmeg and laced with Parmesan cheese.

⅓ c. butter or regular margarine
⅓ c. finely chopped onion
⅓ c. flour
1 tsp. salt
⅛ tsp. pepper
3 c. milk
½ c. grated Parmesan cheese

1/16 tsp. ground nutmeg
2 (7-oz.) cans tuna, drained and flaked
8 oz. wide noodles, cooked and drained
2 (10-oz.) pkg. frozen broccoli spears, cooked and drained

Cut and measure all ingredients before starting to cook.

Melt butter in 12″ skillet or electric frypan over medium heat (300⁰), about 3 minutes.

Add onion and sauté 5 minutes or until tender.

Stir in flour, salt and pepper. Gradually stir in milk. Cook, stirring constantly, until mixture boils and thickens, about 15 minutes.

Stir in Parmesan cheese, nutmeg and tuna. Remove sauce from skillet to a bowl.

Arrange noodles in same skillet. Place broccoli spears on top. Spoon tuna sauce over noodles and broccoli. (Do not stir.)

Cook over low heat (220⁰). Cover and heat 10 minutes or until hot.

Makes 4 to 6 servings.

201/Tuna tetrazzini

• *Preparation time: 9 minutes*
• *Cooking time: 24 minutes*

Tuna casserole fans will like this company version featuring spaghetti, mushrooms, peas and a sprinkle of fresh parsley.

4 tblsp. butter or regular margarine
½ c. finely chopped onion
¼ c. flour
½ tsp. salt
⅛ tsp. pepper
2⅓ c. chicken broth
1 (13-oz.) can evaporated milk
8 oz. broken spaghetti, cooked and drained

2 (7-oz.) cans solid-pack tuna, drained and broken into chunks
1 (4-oz.) can mushroom stems and pieces, drained
1 (10-oz.) pkg. frozen peas, cooked and drained
1 c. grated Parmesan cheese
½ c. chopped fresh parsley

Cut and measure all ingredients before starting to cook.

Melt butter in 12″ skillet or electric frypan over medium heat (300⁰), about 2 minutes.

Add onion and sauté 2 minutes or until tender. Stir in flour, salt and pepper. Gradually stir in chicken broth and evaporated milk. Cook, stirring constantly, until mixture boils and thickens, about 10 minutes.

Stir in spaghetti, tuna, mushrooms, peas, Parmesan cheese and parsley. Toss mixture well so spaghetti is coated.

Reduce heat to low (220⁰). Cover and simmer 10 minutes or until thoroughly heated.

Makes 6 to 8 servings.

202/Bacon fried rice

- *Preparation time: 12 minutes*
- *Cooking time: 21 minutes*

An Americanized version of Chinese fried rice. Bacon adds an interesting flavor to this rice and mushroom mixture.

½ lb. bacon, diced
4 eggs, beaten
⅛ tsp. pepper
¾ c. chopped onion
¾ c. chopped green pepper
1 (4-oz.) can mushroom
   stems and pieces

2 c. cold cooked rice
½ tsp. salt
2 tblsp. chopped fresh
   parsley

Cut and measure all ingredients before starting to cook.

Fry bacon in 10″ skillet over medium heat 10 minutes or until browned. Remove with slotted spoon and drain on paper towels.

Pour bacon drippings into a small bowl. Wash out skillet.

Return 1 tblsp. of the bacon drippings to skillet. Heat over medium heat 1 minute.

Add eggs and pepper to skillet and cook 2 minutes or until set. Remove from skillet.

Return 2 more tblsp. of the bacon drippings to skillet and heat over medium heat 1 minute.

Add onion and green pepper. Sauté 5 minutes.

Stir in undrained mushrooms, rice, salt, parsley and bacon.

Cook and stir 2 minutes. Cut cooked eggs into small pieces and stir into skillet.

Serve with soy sauce, if you wish.

Makes 4 servings.

203/French omelet
with tomato sauce

- *Preparation time: 6 minutes*
- *Cooking time: 48 minutes*

A light, fluffy French-style omelet with an extra-flavorful tomato, mushroom, green pepper and onion sauce.

2 tblsp. cooking oil	1 drop Tabasco sauce
½ c. chopped onion	¼ tsp. salt
½ c. chopped green pepper	⅛ tsp. pepper
1 clove garlic, minced	3 tblsp. butter or regular
1 (8-oz.) can stewed	margarine
tomatoes	8 eggs
1 (4-oz.) can sliced	3 tblsp. milk
mushrooms	¼ tsp. salt
1 (8-oz.) can tomato sauce	⅛ tsp. pepper
½ c. water	Grated Parmesan cheese

Cut and measure all ingredients before starting to cook.

Heat oil in 12″ skillet or electric frypan over medium heat (350º) 5 minutes or until hot.

Add onion, green pepper and garlic. Sauté 7 minutes. Stir in tomatoes, undrained mushrooms, tomato sauce, water, Tabasco sauce, ¼ tsp. salt and ⅛ tsp. pepper. Cook until mixture comes to a boil, about 2 minutes. Reduce heat to low (220º). Simmer, uncovered, 25 minutes. Pour into bowl; set aside.

Melt butter in same skillet over medium heat (350º), about 2 minutes. Beat together eggs, milk, ¼ tsp. salt and ⅛ tsp. pepper in bowl with fork until blended.

Pour egg mixture into skillet. As eggs begin to set around edges, lift edges with spatula and tilt skillet so uncooked portion flows underneath. Continue cooking until egg mixture is set and bottom is lightly browned, about 7 minutes.

Loosen with turner and fold omelet in half. Invert onto warm platter. Pour sauce over all; sprinkle with cheese.

Makes 6 servings.

204/**Stuffed shells**

- *Preparation time: 10 minutes*
- *Cooking time: 51 minutes*

You can serve this Italian favorite as a main course for six, or as a first course for as many as 12. Either way, it's a hit.

2½ qt. water
1 tsp. salt
1 tblsp. cooking oil
8 oz. jumbo stuffing shells
2 c. shredded mozzarella cheese
2 (15-oz.) containers ricotta cheese
½ c. grated Romano cheese

2 eggs, beaten
3 tblsp. chopped fresh parsley
1 tsp. salt
⅛ tsp. pepper
⅛ tsp. ground nutmeg
2 (15½-oz.) jars spaghetti sauce without meat
¼ c. grated Romano cheese

Cut and measure all ingredients before starting to cook.

Heat water and 1 tsp. salt in 12″ skillet or electric frypan over high heat (400°) until it boils, about 8 minutes.

Add oil and shells. Cook 20 minutes, stirring occasionally. Drain in colander and place on paper towels.

Meanwhile, mix together mozzarella cheese, ricotta cheese, ½ c. Romano cheese, eggs, parsley, 1 tsp. salt, pepper and nutmeg in bowl. Fill shells with cheese mixture.

Pour ¾ c. of the spaghetti sauce in bottom of same skillet. Arrange shells in skillet. Pour remaining spaghetti sauce on top. Cook until mixture comes to a boil over medium heat (350°), about 3 minutes.

Reduce heat to low (220°). Cover and simmer 20 minutes. Sprinkle with ¼ c. Romano cheese before serving.

Makes 6 servings.

205/Ratatouille

- *Preparation time: 20 minutes*
- *Cooking time: 57 minutes*

Some prefer this Mediterranean vegetable dish served cold as an accompaniment; others like to feature it as a hot entrée.

2 tblsp. cooking oil
1 c. chopped onion
1 clove garlic, minced
1 lb. eggplant, pared and
  cubed (4¼ c.)
3 medium zucchini, sliced
  (3 c.)
1 green pepper, cut into
  strips

4 tomatoes, peeled and
  chopped
1 tsp. salt
½ tsp. dried basil leaves
½ tsp. dried thyme leaves
¼ tsp. pepper

Cut and measure all ingredients before starting to cook.

Heat oil in 12″ skillet or electric frypan over medium heat (350⁰) 5 minutes or until hot.

Add onion and garlic. Sauté 5 minutes or until tender.

Add eggplant, zucchini, green pepper, tomatoes, salt, basil, thyme and pepper. Cook until mixture comes to a boil, about 2 minutes.

Reduce heat to low (220⁰). Cover and simmer 15 minutes.

Uncover and continue simmering 30 minutes or until vegetables are tender and mixture is thickened.

Makes 8 servings.

206/Asparagus crepes

- *Preparation time: 15 minutes*
- *Cooking time: 43 minutes*

Fresh spring asparagus can make this brunch entrée even more appealing. Increase cooking time accordingly—but don't overcook.

Crepes (recipe follows)
3 tblsp. cooking oil
½ lb. fresh mushrooms, sliced
½ c. chopped onion
1 clove garlic, minced
1 (8-oz.) can stewed tomatoes, cut up
⅓ c. chicken broth
½ tsp. dried tarragon leaves

⅛ tsp. pepper
¼ tsp. Worcestershire sauce
2 drops Tabasco sauce
1 (10-oz.) pkg. frozen asparagus spears, cut into ½" pieces
1 tsp. cornstarch
1 tblsp. water
½ c. pasteurized American process cheese spread

Cut and measure all ingredients before starting to cook. Prepare crepes.

Heat 10″ skillet over medium-high heat 1 minute. Brush skillet with ½ tsp. of the oil. Pour a scant ½ c. crepe batter into skillet, tilting to coat entire bottom surface of skillet. Bake 2 minutes. Turn over and bake 2 minutes more or until browned. Repeat with remaining batter and oil, making 5 more crepes, about 20 minutes. Keep crepes warm.

Heat 2 tblsp. oil in same skillet over medium-high heat, about 2 minutes. Add mushrooms, onion and garlic. Sauté 5 minutes. Stir in next 6 ingredients. Cook 5 minutes. Add asparagus and cook 3 minutes more. Combine cornstarch and water in bowl. Stir into skillet. Cook until it boils, about 1 minute. Boil 1 minute. Add cheese spread and stir until blended, about 1 minute. Remove from heat. Arrange one-sixth of asparagus filling on each crepe and roll up.

Makes 6 crepes.

Crepes: Combine ¾ c. sifted flour, ¼ tsp. salt, 1 c. milk and 2 eggs in bowl. Beat with rotary beater until smooth.

Index

Curried
   chicken skillet, 22
   pork with rice, 65
   turkey with rice, 26

D

Dill beef rolls, 174
Double cheese macaroni, 18
Dried beef, *see* Beef

E

Easy
   barbecue buns, 36
   hamburger stroganoff, 2
   macaroni skillet, 38
Egg(s)
   and chipped beef, Creamed, 49
   and vegetables provencale, 161
   Bacon potato puff, 160
   Country breakfast skillet, 159
   foo yung, Shrimp, 88
   French omelet with tomato
      sauce, 203
   Hash and, 123
   Low-cal vegetable omelet, 48
   puff, Cheesy, 47
   Western sandwiches, 46
Eggplant
   Beef with, 8
   Ratatouille, 205
   -rice skillet, 173
   stacks with spaghetti sauce,
      33
Elegant beef fillets, 166
Enchilada casserole, 171

F

Family-style stroganoff, 105
Fish, *see also* names of fish
Four-layer skillet dinner, 112

Frankfurter(s), *see also*
      Hot dogs
   Barbecued beans with, 45
   Beans and, 41
   Corn meal pancakes with, 156
   Quick bean soup, 44
   skillet, Noodle, 42
French
   omelet with tomato sauce, 203
   -style bean casserole, 180

G

Gardener's skillet supper, 110
German skillet dinner, 99
Ginger chicken, 83
Green bean(s), *see* Bean(s)
Grilled
   ham salad sandwiches, 21
   tuna sandwiches, 29
Ground beef, *see also* Beef,
      Hamburger(s), Meatball(s),
      Meat loaf(ves)

H

Haddock
   chowder, Squash and, 198
   Landlubber's seafood
      chowder, 145
   Spaghetti with, 144
   Sweet-and-sour, 197
Ham, *see* Pork
Hamburger(s), *see also* Beef,
      Meatball(s), Meat loaf(ves)
   broccoli skillet, 64
   Corn-stuffed, 5
   Home-style, 118
   pie, 13
   -potato skillet, 6
   skillet, Upside-down, 104
   stir-fry, 61

Poultry, *see* Chicken, Turkey

Q

Quick
  bean soup, 44
  bean supper, 35
  -cook vegetable scallop, 155
  ham-macaroni skillet, 20
  salmon chowder, 147

R

Rancher's beef stew, 11
Ratatouille, 205
Reuben sandwiches, 39
Rice
  Bacon fried, 202
  Beef
    liver in spicy sauce, 121
    with onions and
      zucchini, 55
    with pea pods, 58
  California stir-fried
    chicken, 76
  Cheesy
    beef with, 109
    creamed shrimp, 27
  Chicken
    and, 23
    chop suey, 81
    fried, 85
    vegetable stir-fry, 82
    with green beans, 84
  Chinese
    beef with vegetables, 54
    beef with water chestnuts,
      60
    pork with vegetables, 69
    -style chicken salad, 80
  Classic sukiyaki, 56

Creamed ham with spinach
  and, 131
Curried
  pork with, 65
  turkey with, 26
Dill beef rolls, 174
Ground beef sukiyaki, 62
Ham strips in tomato
  sauce, 134
Mary's chicken in honey
  sauce, 192
Oriental
  pepper steak, 59
  tuna, 89
Polynesian meatballs, 175
Porcupine meatballs, 120
Pork
  -broccoli stir-fry, 71
  fried, 66
Shrimp with asparagus, 87
skillet, Eggplant-, 173
soup, Hearty tomato, 3
Spanish shrimp with, 199
Stir-fried almond chicken, 77
Sweet-and-sour
  chicken, 75
  fish, 197
  ham with pineapple, 73
  pork, 70
  turkey, 86

S

Salad(s)
  Chinese-style chicken, 80
  Old-fashioned potato, 164
  Viennese potato, 163
Salmon
  chowder, Quick, 147
Sandwich(es)
  Barbecued beef, 113

214

squash and zucchini, 52
zucchini with beef, 16
Swedish meatballs with
   noodles, 172
Sweet-and-sour
   chicken, 75
   fish, 197
   ham with pineapple, 73
   pork, 70
   spareribs, 181
   turkey, 86
Sweet potatoes
   and ham patties, Candied, 130
Swiss steak elegante, 170

T
Tuna
   burgers with noodles, 146
   casserole with almonds, 28
   divan, 200
   Oriental, 89
   sandwiches, Grilled, 29
   tetrazzini, 201
Tomato(es)
   and bacon pizza with home-
      made crust, 157
   Parmesan zucchini and, 162
   rice soup, Hearty, 3
Turkey
   Monte Cristo sandwiches, 25
   Sweet-and-sour, 86
   with rice, Curried, 26

U
Upside-down
   corned beef hash, 122
   hamburger skillet, 104
   sausage 'n' stuffing, 150

V
Veal Parmesan, 177
Vegetable(s)
   Chicken with garden, 78
   Chinese beef with, 54
   Chinese pork with, 69
   dumpling soup, 96
   Meat loaf and, 102
   omelet, Low-cal, 48
   Oriental stir-fried, 90
   Oriental-style pork and, 67
   Provencale, Eggs and, 161
   scallop, Quick-cook, 155
   stir-fry, Chicken, 82
Viennese potato salad, 163

W
Wagon-wheel sausage supper,
   148
Welsh rabbit, 50
Western sandwiches, 46
Western-style beans, 7

Z
Zucchini
   and tomatoes, Parmesan, 162
   Beef with onions and, 55
   Creole-style chicken, 139
   Italian-style, 30
   Ratatouille, 205
   Spanish-style squash, 12
   Summer squash and, 52
   supper, Spicy, 97
   with beef, Summer, 16
   with noodles, Broccoli and, 51
   with sausage and cheese, 151